Dear Joanne —
You are one of my
favorite readers!
I'm looking forward to
hearing your comments!
Love, D

A Mango for the Teacher

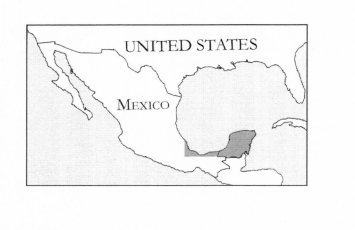

UNITED STATES

MEXICO

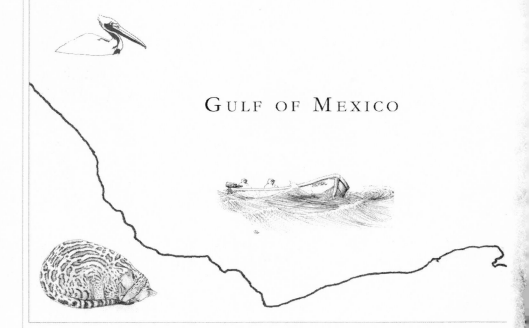

GULF OF MEXICO

A Mango for the Teacher

Running the Beach
and Running a School
In Cancún's Early Days

Deborah Frisch

Illustrations by Arturo Avila

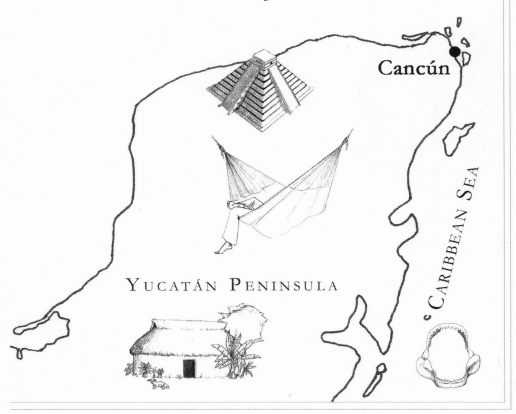

Cancún

CARIBBEAN SEA

YUCATÁN PENINSULA

To Leonora, Uncle Arturo, and Moses, for preparing me for *aventura*.

Published by Xicalango Press
www.xicalangopress.com
www.deborahfrisch.com

First Edition 10 9 8 7 6 5 4 3 2 1

ACKNOWLEDGEMENTS

This book would never have been written without the guidance and encouragement of Bill Hyman, my instructor in the Monday Memoir Class at Albany Senior Center in California, and of my talented classmates there. The first five or six chapters were written for Debra Ratner's class at the same center. Like Bill, Debra is an outstanding teacher, and was the final editor of my manuscript.

Writing consultant Dorothy Wall gave me valuable assistance and reassurance about the project early on; Anne Fox, editor *extraordinaire* of the California Writers Club, Berkeley Branch, was a guide and a taskmaster when that was needed.

The sharp eyes of my friend Lucille Bellucci gave the manuscript one last careful reading. Graphics for the book, including the cover, are the work of excellent graphic designers Alfredo Rivas, Bruce Hopkins, and Ralph Granich. Kristen Caven of Cowgirl Creative was responsible for the innovative use of graphics in the book design.

I am grateful to my son Arturo for his poignant illustrations, and for reminding me of aspects of the story that I had forgotten. To the friends who appear in these pages, I consider myself lucky to continue friendships with you after so many years. My son Lee provided needed computer advice. My daughter-in-law Ranjana, aside from giving me editorial help, showed pride and enthusiasm for the project; this meant the world to me. In addition, I appreciate my husband David more than ever when I think of how his critical thinking and reading have contributed to this book.

Author's Note: The names of many people who figure in this memoir have been changed.

PROLOGUE

"Welcome to Sexual Saturday—no, no, I meant *Social Friday!*"
said Roddy, the teacher from Belize.

Once the laughter ebbed and the students' faces relaxed in
smiles, our weekly sing-along began. Seventy or more of us were
crowded into a single classroom at Escuela Xicalango, the English
language school for adults I had founded two years earlier, in 1976.
Its home was an L-shaped brick house on Avenue Nader, one
block from Avenue Tulúm.

"*Míranos,*" one student nudged another. "Look at us, we're
packed in here like rice." Eighteen sat in sturdy blue chairs around
a long, white conference table; the others stood elbow to sweaty
elbow behind the seated students. Overhead two large ceiling fans
whirred, sending aloft the scent of alcohol from the mimeographed
song sheets the students held.

First, the advanced students translated the song of the week,
Billy Joel's "My Life," into Spanish. Then the teachers took turns
reading lyrics aloud for the students to repeat. Harry, a former
backup man for a top soul singer, read the song with such feeling
you'd think he had written it himself. His sexy baritone had the
young women glancing at each other and giggling.

When Loretta, the redheaded teacher from Tennessee, recited
the words, students repeated "the A-MUR-i-cun way."

I grew up in Brooklyn and Long Island; whenever the students
repeated after me, the echoes of Flatbush Avenue made me smile.

The gossip in Cancún had it that Escuela Xicalango was *bueno,
bonito y barato*, good, good-looking and cheap. All true. Our tuition
was around one US dollar per day, so we were not out of range for
middle and low-income people. Since we were considered the best
English school in town, students from the upper economic levels
attended too. That's why we had bank officers practicing questions
and answers with handicraft salesmen, and the mayor's son with
the mechanic's daughter.

The student body ranged in age from sixteen to over seventy and hailed from every region of Mexico, plus the odd Spaniard or Central American. The teaching staff was also diverse in origin, age and professional background. But regardless of our differences, we were united in the enterprise of teaching and learning English, and singing songs we cared about—we roared those songs! The teachers hammed it up, the students ate it up—we sang with heart and belly and soul.

Some Fridays we rocked with the Stones while young men drummed on the table. I loved to sing "I Will Survive," and I was not alone. Women shimmied their shoulders in their tight tank tops singing "Lady Marmalade" while men pumped their arms in the air à la John Travolta. But Billy Joel's "My Life" had special significance: as the song says, we had all "closed up shop" to come to Cancún. Crammed shoulder to shoulder, we sang out, "This is *my* life!"

Morning classes over, I locked the door to the school and headed upstairs to my bedroom. Undressing in front of the mirror, I stared critically at my reflection. "Can I get away with the bikini?" My tanned tummy hardly stuck out at all. "Bikini it *is!*" I decided, and stepped into it. Then I slathered on Coppertone #4, threw a beach dress on top, and drove off singing, toward *my* beach.

It was noon when I started running, pelicans soaring overhead. I ran where the sand was packed hard, where the waves recede. The midday horizon was lavender, shading upward to azure. The sea was like turquoise ginger ale, transparent, effervescent.

On my two miles of broad sun-bleached beach I saw no one. While I ran, ideas came to me like water birds in flight: they appeared tiny and indistinct on the horizon, but soon I could see them in detail. I found myself inventing a game to practice the afternoon's lesson; other days a poem or story might take shape in my mind. My dad also wrote stories—what would he be doing this time of day in New York, I wondered.

The wind was out of the south, and I was running against it. My eyes focused on my turning point, the only building on the beach. From here it was a tiny beige rectangle, but up close you could see its glossy mahogany beams. It was an extravagant three-story structure with Mayan arches and stone stairways, a beach residence of the president of Mexico. By the time I reached the "Casa Maya," I felt like a roasted peanut in my green bikini, firm and brown, oily and salty.

Now I veered from the water's edge and plunged into waves through foam thick as whipped cream. I swam hard until I passed the breakers. On a sandbar I stood on tiptoes, panting. Squadrons of small fish cruised past my knees; coral-colored shells shifted around my feet.

Cool again, I swam and waded to the beach, then began running toward my starting point, the southernmost hotel on ten miles of solitary shoreline. With the wind behind me, I sailed along to the pace of the morning's tune.

From the crest of a wave, a school of the gleaming baitfish known as ballyhoo leapt into the air, all silver sides as they turned in unison. They dove, but I could still see them swimming inside the curl. The pelicans, wingtips upturned, hovered above. Then the fish jumped from the water again, chaotically this time. A split second later a huge toothy snout broke through the curl and came surfing toward me. It was a gigantic barracuda, the cause of this havoc. Its hatchet face and half its thick cylinder of a body protruded from a glassy wave with a dozen silver ballyhoo thrashing in its jaws.

Life and death, beauty and blood—what a spectacle! I turned in all directions, wild to shout to someone, "Look at that!" But as far as I could see, there was no one to shout to; there was no one on the beach but me.

For as many reasons as the water has waves, I left Cancún in 1988, never to reside there again. Escuela Xicalango floundered along until the year 2000, when I sold it to a couple that opened a Spanish language school in its place.

During a visit in the spring of 2009, I could barely walk my stretch of ocean beach, what with the erosion, the drop-offs and expanses of jagged rock. Hotels, nearly two hundred and fifty of them, jammed the shoreline. Without the buffer of sand, the sea was rapidly undermining the hotels and the fortune they represent for Mexico.

In response, that fall the federal government dug a "grand canyon" in the ocean floor two miles west of Cozumel and dumped the 178.5 million cubic feet of sand where Cancún's beach used to be. It's holding, for now. When I visited in 2010, and looked out across the broad beach at the water, the view was dazzling.

Just as the beach has been remade, so has the peninsula. The entire Mayan region has endured a sea change, brought about by the phenomenal growth of tourism. But the extraordinary sights, tastes and personalities, what I longed to share decades ago, are still there, in remote corners or under the surface. *Ven conmigo,* come with me, back to the days when every grain of sand was new, when my friends and I wondered whether Cancún would ever catch on....

 *1* **Excessed**

"Excessed?" I read aloud from the New York City Board of Education's letter, dated June 3rd, 1975. It began:

Dear Ms. Frisch,
Due to budgetary constraints, teachers with less than one year at a school site will be excessed as of…

"Excessed isn't even a word!" I exclaimed to no one; I was alone on the stoop of my Brooklyn brownstone apartment. But of course I understood what it meant. After all, I was twenty-seven, with a master's degree in teaching. For a diploma from the School of Education, mastery of bureaucratic jargon was required. Besides, this was my third such letter from the Board in two years.

A headline in my neighbor's *New York Times* on the steps

caught my eye: "CITY CUTS 40,000." I sat down on the stoop beside the newspaper, deciding whether to ball the Board's letter up and pitch it out into Clinton Street or take a match to it.

My mother and my Aunt Eileen were both editors—the three of us would have had great fun lampooning the Board's Newspeak—but they were gone. And my uncle, the one I called "Tío Arturo" because he loved to horse around with my mom and me in Spanish, was gone too. Propped up in his hospital bed searching the classifieds, he had found me this last job.

They were my favorites, my mom, my aunt and uncle, and they had left me, but they hadn't left me destitute. Two and a half years earlier, when I was twenty-four, my mom's will had provided me with $900, enough for four months of intensive Spanish classes in Mexico, with time off for bad behavior.

Uncle Arturo's will had left me more than enough money for another getaway, this time in a car.

And so, on the day after the school year ended, my friend Sandra and I drove out of the city across the Verrazano Bridge, and then south, toward the border.

Sandra was twenty-five, "*una niñita*," a little girl, I kidded her. She was a good six inches taller than I, big-boned, with a long, pale face and freckles. She wore baggy overall-shorts and twisted her reddish hair into an unruly knot at the back of her head. The way she raised her chin and asked, "Yeah?" to keep you talking, the one eyebrow that flew up when something sounded fishy: pure Brooklyn charm. We were in the same boat, she and I; no boyfriends, no jobs, and ready to see what life had to offer beyond the five boroughs.

2 The Green Semiautomatic

The car was a second-hand kelly-green semiautomatic VW beetle, purchased with a couple of thousand dollars inherited from Uncle Arturo—had he been around, his head would have been under that rear hood before any money changed hands. Volkswagen sold this model in the late 'sixties and early 'seventies; it had a gearshift but no clutch pedal. Their ads claimed, "Drive it for a few days and it *becomes* automatic."

We traveled south smoothly as a leaf on a stream. Sometimes Sandra pushed the seat back and drove while I assembled sandwiches and played Celia Cruz cassettes. A few hours later I would take the wheel while Sandra handed me pieces of *rugelach* pastry her mom had baked for our trip. Joni Mitchell was Sandra's favorite music, along with the Beatles and Bob Marley.

We made a deal: anytime we disagreed about routes, or whether the singer was John or Paul, or how far ahead the next gas station might be, we would make a bet. The loser would pick up the dinner check. New things to bet on popped up every day.

In Atlanta Sandra and I had a rollicking time rafting the Chattahoochee River with my brother. A day later we stopped for an evening with the Preservation Hall Jazz Band in New Orleans, where, when we asked the octogenarian master musicians to sign their records, they kissed our hands.

But at the border crossing at Laredo the good times stopped rolling. There we sat sweating for hours in a logjam of cars and trucks with Mexican license plates.

Women and children threaded among the stopped cars, uncovering baskets of moist little tacos called *sudados* beside each driver. They pushed them through the open windows, and aromas of chile, of cumin and onions filled the car. Sandra wouldn't try any, but the first one I ate was hot and tender, juicy and spicy. The vendor had made them herself that morning, she said. I bought two more from her. Then I bought one from a boy who seemed to have stepped out of a Diego Rivera painting, and another from a voluble teenager with a striped *reboso* over her basket.

"¡*Cuidado*, watch out with the tongue tacos!" she joked in Spanish, "They make you talk too much—like me!"

"*Sudados* are supposed to 'sweat' in the basket," I jabbered to Sandra, "it moistens the tortillas and blends the flavors." I went on, listing all my favorite fillings and describing the variety of garnishes and salsas to go with them.

"I can't eat that," Sandra said, inverting her customary smile. "I'll get sick."

"Everywhere in Mexico," I told her, "people practically *live* on street food. The vendors have to keep clean—otherwise their customers won't come back. Have a bite." I paid with pesos we had just bought from the best-looking of the black marketeers standing in the median strip. I held a blue twenty-peso bill up to the light to show Sandra the watermark; backlit, Benito Juárez's noble face magically appeared.

How did I know these things? My first time in Mexico, in 1972, I had spent over four months in intensive Spanish classes, and my extracurricular activities were even more intensive. During my home stay with a family in Chapalita, Guadalajara, the mom had cast me in the role of chaperone for her eldest daughters, but she hadn't cast anyone as chaperone for me.

I'd been learning the Mexican ropes in Guadalajara for two months when Moses, my best friend from City College, took me up on a dare: he called me at the family's home, and left a message with a local phone number. It was a thrill to find him there and introduce him to a city and a culture I now knew much about.

The next day Moses and I rented a car and drove to Puerta Vallarta. From there a short boat trip to Yelapa ushered us into a night of the iguana to rival Liz and Richard's. Conveniently, my course in Guadalajara had just ended, and I felt ready to find my way in Mexico City. I exchanged *abrazos y besos* (hugs and kisses) with the Chapalita family, and then Moses and I took off for the capital. He had to be back at work in New York within a few days. At a café on the road, a trio of American girls who lived in Mexico City started talking with us. They were guests at the bachelor pad of some university students. They invited me to join them, and there, my instruction had continued.

At the border in Laredo with Sandra, our semiautomatic finally came abreast of the small building housing Mexican Customs and Immigration. Sandra and I got out of the car and walked into the office. Several smiling young men in uniform carefully examined our papers, the car's papers, Sandra's long legs and my flowered tank top. I had the feeling they would have been delighted to abandon their stations and escort us into their country.

In fact, once we were on the Mexican side of the border, everything and everybody seemed so hot and haphazard—how was it possible that nothing more than a dry excuse for a river separated two different worlds?

Then the haphazard part crystallized. Although a thick red line on the map represented a major highway between Nuevo Laredo and Monterrey, the dusty road-under-construction that lay ahead was crisscrossed with yellow-and-black *DESVIACION* (detour) and *NO HAY PASO* (No Through Road) signs, with nameless byways taking off with no discernable destination. I hadn't expected our route to expire the instant we crossed the border. In mounting panic I drove through dust and truck traffic on the faintest trace of a road, braking often to ponder the signs. They used abbreviations that meant nothing to me and referred to place names we couldn't locate on the map.

Whenever we stopped, though, a large van with the tan-and-red logo of Raleigh cigarettes paused behind us. "They're following us!" Sandra exclaimed, looking out the dusty back window at the grinning driver in dark glasses and his tall, husky passenger. "Why are they following us?"

"Maybe they're going to Monterrey too," I proposed uneasily, "and they know the road. I'm *glad* they're staying close."

"Huhn!" Sandra sniffed.

A little while later Sandra raised one eyebrow at me. "That van is probably packed to the roof with American girls who got lost on this road." It seemed she had cast me as an ally of the Raleigh's men. This wasn't what I wanted on my first day back in Mexico.

I kept driving, hunched over the wheel like Quasimodo. After many miles, the van pulled up alongside us. From this distance Sir Walter Raleigh—the giant, bearded face in the ad emblazoned on the truck—leered at me. I managed to croak a one-word question at the driver: "*¿Monterrey?*" He nodded his black mane vigorously and his sunglasses flashed in the sun; beside him the large man with the military haircut winked at me.

With me doing all the driving, we followed *los Señores Raleigh* for hours more, over washboard road in construction, newly laid gravel that pinged on the bottom of the semi, unmarked fresh asphalt where ours was the second set of tire tracks. When both vehicles made a pit stop at a PEMEX *gasolinera*, we exchanged tight smiles while *Los Raleighs* headed to the *HOMBRES*, and we to *MUJERES*. I wondered if *HOMBRES* could possibly be as appalling as *MUJERES*. Sandra wondered if they were leading us to the Raleigh corporate lair.

I kept referring to the men as "our escorts," but Sandra wouldn't stop speculating about what favors these escorts might ask.

And when we finally parked our dust-crusted Beetle beside their van in the parking lot of a Mongolian barbecue on the outskirts of Monterrey, Sandra was right—they *did* want something from us: they wanted us to join them for dinner. In Spanish, English and sign language, we relieved the tension of the drive with spareribs and chow mein. We taught the men how to use chopsticks, and toasted each other Mexican-style, *arriba, abajo, al centro, y adentro* (above, below, in the middle and down the hatch) after our hard day on the road together. Then we found one room in a nearby motel, and they found another. *Muchas gracias* was what we gave *los Raleighs* as thanks for guiding us into Mexico.

3   *Una Cosa Fácil*

My seatmate on my first flight to Mexico, back in September of 1972, spoke *ni papa de inglés*, not a single word. But her eyes gleamed like chocolate melting in a pot as she bubbled about Guadalajara, the city where I would spend the next few months. "*Déborah*," Marielena assured me in Spanish, "you will *adore* it here!" She clasped my hand with soft fingers adorned with diamonds. I was delighted with her show of affection, and with how well I understood her. The University was not far from the hotel I had booked, Marielena said. It would be *una cosa fácil,* easy, to get there.

Early in the morning I brushed my waist-length light-brown hair in the hotel mirror, admiring my looks and my pluckiness. I knew what I was doing here in Mexico.

Out on the sidewalk by nine in the morning, I followed the directions Marielena had given me. But where were those landmarks she had described? Soon I asked for help. "*¿La Universidad?*" a woman repeated my question. "Walk two blocks, and then turn right at the *semáforo*." Is that really what she said? Turn at the punctuation mark?

The next person advised me to take a #6 bus that stopped at a "*glorieta*." What in God's name was a *glorieta*? I had a pocket dictionary with me, but this word was not in it. I asked, too, but people responded by making funny whirling motions with their hands.

Around four in the sweltering afternoon, I waved my arms, demanding that the bus driver let me off my third bus of the day, on a road through a field where cows grazed. "How did this happen? And *now* what will I do…?" I sobbed at intervals on my long trek toward the buildings of downtown.

How had it happened? The driver of the taxi I finally found asked me, *"¿La Universidad de Guadalajara, o La Universidad Autónoma?"* I had been following directions toward one university and then the other all day. They were located at opposite ends of the city. I had never heard that there were two universities.

A *glorieta* is a traffic circle, I soon learned, a common feature in the Mexican traffic system. And a *semáforo* is a traffic light, of course: two dots, one above and one below.

4 *The Plunge*

Back in the fall of 1972, I followed the two months of intensive Spanish classes in Guadalajara with two more months of classes in Mexico City. I was sharing an apartment across the street from the racetrack with three American girls. One evening a young man called to speak with Ariel, one of the girls. She wasn't at home, but he and I had fun on the phone for an hour or more.

"I *hated* English in school," he moaned through the receiver in Spanish, "I can't speak it *at all*." Well, that was convenient for me; I was trying to practice my Spanish day and night. We arranged to meet the next night in front of the Cine Reforma.

Paco and I liked each other immediately. He was a James Dean look-alike built on a small scale, cheery and enthusiastic about everything Mexican, and about me, too. At thirty he owned and managed his own business, an office-furniture factory. In his cool little sky-blue Fiat sports car he would wait for me in it in front of the Instituto Mexicano-Americano when my Spanish classes were letting out.

It didn't take long before Paco asked me to join him and two others on a Christmas vacation jaunt to Isla Mujeres and Cozumel. I didn't know where those places were, but nevertheless I'm sure I answered, *"¡Cómo no!"*

Before we left on our trip, I was Paco's date at his factory's Christmas party. There I helped him give out presents to two or three dozen employees and their children. They seemed genuinely fond of him, and they treated me like the crown princess.

On the way back to my apartment, I told Paco how touched I'd felt by the reception I got at the party. This led Paco to tell me about being raised by employees at his difficult mother's sweater factory, and by *campesinos* at his demanding father's ranch. Having learned from his parents about managing businesses, at the age of twenty-seven he was offered the contract with which he started the factory. He described the scene: he was in his bathing suit, at a swimming pool in Acapulco. I was very impressed with him, and with the way he squinted those sexy James Dean eyes at me. At my front door he began talking about marriage—not a proposal exactly, more an idea to keep in mind while we traveled.

The names of the places we were to visit, Cozumel and Isla Mujeres, appeared on my map in minuscule blue print. I discovered they were islands off the coast of the *Territorio de Quintana Roo*. This enormous province lacked the requisite population for statehood: 25,000 people.

The trip was not easy. Although a new highway had recently opened, Paco insisted on driving the old scenic route and taking car ferries across lagoons and rivers. Because it was holiday season, the ferries were at capacity, and we were on the road for five or six long days. After being turned away from an overcrowded ferry to Isla Mujeres, we wandered south a bit, and came upon a construction bridge that crossed a canal. It bore a hand-painted wooden sign tilted at a crazy angle; the only word on the sign was "CAN-CUN."

Cramped with another woman in the back seat of Paco's Volkswagen bug while the men sat in front, I was wound up tighter than a rubber-band ball; all four of us reeked of sweat and irritability. Slowly we drove over the crude wooden bridge and followed a sandy track to its end at a point of rocks. We had reached Punta Cancún, where Hotel Camino Real now stands. What I saw there drove me wild; never had I imagined frothy whitecaps on rolling turquoise waves.

Dropping shorts to the sand and whooping like Tarzans and Janes, we four plunged into the surf in our underwear. The water was delicious, bracing but not cold. Waves were breaking in every direction, and pelicans dove between us. "*This* is where I want to live!" I cried out.

"Oh really, Déborah?" Paco laughed. "Where?" My gaze followed his, up and down the beach. There was not one hint of a village, much less a resort. In fact, there was no one in sight. Still, I thought, someone had built that bridge. Far to the south I spied a parked tractor, its snub nose pointing up a dune. This place was a mystery as dense as the jungle that lay behind the beach. We speculated about Can-Cun all the way back to Mexico City.

The Volkswagen we had traveled in was Paco's. Nearly all the decisions *en route* were Paco's. When we returned to Mexico City, the students' apartment where I had stayed was no longer available, and soon I was living at Paco's. I felt as if I were still captive in that little VW bug.

Then, shortly after our return, a phone conversation with my dad in New York revealed that he was scheduled for prostate surgery. I'd better fly back to help him, I decided, and get away from Paco for a while.

A week or so after my father's surgery, Paco called to say he was coming to visit. He arrived serendipitously, I thought, just hours before a dance party at a friend's East Village apartment. There another friend, an African-American named Brandon, led me out on the floor to dance. Just as I was pointing out my Mexican boyfriend to Brandon, Paco cut in, grasping my wrist so hard I groaned. We argued in the next room, and his entire stay was tainted by the incident. Paco returned to Mexico City angry and alone. I went back to NYU, to my ESL program and my editorial job for the Dean of the Graduate School.

About a year later, during a lunch break in the Dean's office, I read in *Time* magazine that a beach called "Cancún" was slated to be the next Mexican hotspot. Those infallible new computers had "scientifically" selected this beach for its beauty, its "air-conditioned sand" and its proximity to the ruins of Tulúm and Chichén Itzá.

"A resort in Cancún!" I shouted, astonishing my office companions. "They will need English teachers!" I might as well have been speaking Mayan, for all the comprehension in their faces.

5 *South from Monterrey*

The morning after the day with *los Señores Raleigh*, as soon as Sandra, the green semiautomatic and I were south of Monterrey, the road was better marked. The towns and villages we passed seemed more modern. We no longer saw huge agave cactuses hung with colorful shirts and dresses drying in the sun, nor did the locals of this region keep burros tied up beside adobe houses.

At a roadside restaurant I returned the bilingual breakfast menu to the waitress with some penciled corrections, including "Orange juice" instead of "Orange jews." When we asked for our bill, the waitress smiled, "No charge." What a perk! I started editing every menu that was handed to me.

A few days later, well fed and confident, we entered gargantuan Mexico City, known in Spanish as D.F., for *distrito federal,* or *disastro federal.*

Before leaving Brooklyn I had called Paco, the ex-boyfriend who had taken me to Cancún in '72. He kindly invited Sandra and me to stay at his apartment in the San Jerónimo district of Mexico City for a couple of days. I hadn't expected him to remember that the day we'd get there was my birthday, but shortly after we arrived, so did the party. Paco's Argentine friend was playing the guitar and singing *"Gracias a la Vida,"* and later *"Las Mañanitas,"* the Mexican birthday song. There was turkey in *mole* and a big, pink-and-green star piñata.

A family from New York, new friends of mine, showed up at the party too. I had met Rahim, an Iraqi-Jewish artist, at a friend's place in NYC. When I described my upcoming trip to him, he said that he, his wife and teenaged son and daughter would meet Sandra and me in Mexico City. I hadn't believed him, but there they were, already buddy-buddy with Paco and the rest.

Of course there was a piñata, and the birthday girl was the first one to be blindfolded and spun around and around. As soon as they handed me the bat, everyone began shouting *"¡Arriba, arriba!"* when the piñata was really *abajo*, and *"¡A la derecha!"* when a point was poking me on the left. Removing the bandana after several hard swings that never connected, I looked around me at the rowdy, affectionate crowd of friends. Now I began to understand what it meant to be an Honored Guest.

Reina, Paco's maid, beribboned braids wrapped around her head, had prepared the rich *mole* for the party. At the same time, she was preparing to leave for the festival of her mountain town, Juxtlahuaca, Oaxaca. After we talked for a little while, she invited Sandra and me to go, too—that way we'd be in on the festival, and she'd get a ride there, too. Paco tended toward enthusiasm about Mexican customs in general, but this festival he had described as *"¡IN-cre-EEE-ble—* incredible!!*"* We three women set off to Oaxaca together several days later.

Sandra and I shared the challenging drive into the mountains. After some seven hours, the last three winding through the Sierra Mixteca, we entered the tiled-roof town of Juxtlahuaca. Reina directed me up a steep, pitted dirt road to her house, in front of which was a ditch that I promptly drove my two right wheels into.

"HA HA HA HA ha ha ha," laughed a dozen cousins as they streamed out of Reina's neat masonry house. Neighbors joined them, and, led by a single tall cousin, they lifted the green semi out of the ditch in no time. "Come in and have something to eat!" everyone yelled.

Reina's grandmother, maroon ribbons threaded through her white braids and a face creased like a raisin, sat on folded knees on a mat on the tile floor, back straight as a broomstick. From her mat she shouted instructions in Mixtec at several young women, and plates with gigantic quesadillas and warm bowls of a foamy light-brown beverage called *tejate* were set before us.

Soon after, we spread our sleeping bags atop woven palm mats on the floor. There we bedded down among a dozen young people, all freshly arrived from the cities where they worked, just in time for Juxtlahuaca's festival.

Around dawn I awoke to find the dozen had multiplied—many more nephews, nieces and grandkids had arrived by bus, car or burro throughout the night to lie down beside us. How many? Reina taught me a Mexican pun: *sin cuenta* means countless, while *cinquenta* means fifty, and that's how many relatives were now staying there, *sin cuenta*. In the middle of the night I had to step carefully over and around the sleeping crowd if I wanted to use the outhouse.

And indeed, who would want to miss such a festival? Sandra and I watched as the family dolled up their pink-and-black pig with yellow paper streamers flowing from the tufts of his ears, a purple crepe-paper frill around his neck and a red bow on his tail. Then we sat on the steps just above the ditch in front of the house, waiting for the *Procesión de los Animales* to pass. Shortly, a French horn, a beat-up trombone and a big bass drum came booming down the unpaved street, leading a fashion show of accessorized turkeys, goats, pigs and calves. Our pretty piggie joined the ranks at a cousin's urging, and with a passel of family, we strutted beside it to the community center.

This was a large quadrangle of adobe buildings with tile roofs. In the courtyard in front of the kitchen, all the animals were slaughtered in short order. Had I been thinking that they were just going to parade them around and then let them go home again? After seeing the blood burst from the throat of a screeching calf, Sandra and I decided to leave.

But squeamishness didn't keep us from returning to eat the rich meals produced at *la communidad*. Sitting on benches at long wooden tables, everyone present ate and drank royally, for all the days and nights of the festival.

The dancing was impressive too. A dense circle of locals watched as costumed performers danced the story of the *Moros* and the *Cristianos*, a re-enactment of Spanish victories over the Moors. "You know," Sandra whispered to me, "I think we're the only tourists here." That wasn't hard to see; she was nearly a head taller than anyone else in the crowd. Except perhaps for the Devil dancer, with genuine bull's horns protruding from his oversized, scowling red mask. Then that Devil turned to look directly at Sandra and me. No, it was *me* he was staring at! He strode out of the center of the circle, cracking his whip on the ground.

"*¡JAMÁS!*" he screamed at me in front of the entire town, "NEVER drive your car into that DITCH again!" The whole community roared with laughter. It was as if I were another daughter of the town, come back for the festival and due for a good ribbing. Sandra looked at me for explanation, but I couldn't manage one; I was laughing too hard.

In New York I'd worn blue jeans and a brown leather jacket, my long brown hair falling straight down my shoulders. Once I overheard someone ask who I was, and someone else respond, "Debby? Oh, she's one of those girls over there with long brown hair and a leather jacket." On this trip awareness was growing in me—here, there was no one else like me. Sandra was friendly to people and they were friendly back, but I could talk to them. For these people, and for me, this communication was a miracle. People often asked where we were from, and when they repeated, *"Nueva Yor,"* it was with admiration. When children saw my camera, they hollered, *"Retrátame!* Take my picture!" My sense of belonging in this country, of being a person everyone wanted to know—each encounter strengthened this feeling.

After two days of festival, we drove back down the mountain and through the Sierra Mixteca to reconnoiter with Rahim and his family in Oaxaca. A festival was in progress there too, the Guelaguetza, a traditional gathering of Oaxacan dancers from each of its thirteen indigenous regions. Today the Guelaguetza is held in a stadium and costs a bundle to attend, and it's well worth it too, but in '75 it was held in the Plaza, for free.

Rahim's wife Sylvia, a little red-haired livewire, had been goading me since we first talked—"You're going to teach in Mexico? I'll believe it when I see it!" At the Hotel California, our headquarters in Oaxaca, I asked the receptionist if they would lend me a typewriter to type up a résumé in Spanish. Not only did they lend it to me, the whole staff thought my writing was hilarious, and edited it with me over and over. After retyping it twice or more, the résumé finally sounded convincing. I was the English teacher Cancún needed.

From Oaxaca, Sylvia, Rahim and family flew back to New York, while the green semiautomatic rolled along like mariachi music. In San Cristóbal de las Casas, at Na Balam, a foundation organized to preserve indigenous cultures, people told us about a festival in the nearby highlands town of Zinacantán. Arriving there, we saw dozens of men clothed in pink-striped ponchos, white shorts and conical straw hats with multicolored ribbons; they were heading up a hill on a road too bumpy for the car. Once we parked, Sandra protested, "We can't go that way, it's only the men!" But I followed them, and she followed me. To the basketball court, where they began what seemed to be a basketball tournament.

After we watched a little while, Rahim's nephew Sayeed and his friend Naeem appeared with a boom box. Shortly the basketball game morphed into a dance, four young New Yorkers with one hundred Zinacantecos and Chamulas. When it started drizzling, Sayeed made his tee shirt into a turban on his head, to everyone's amusement. I stopped dancing to take a picture, but instantly two men grabbed me by the elbows. It seemed they were going to take my camera away. Sandra and I went into a panic. But as soon as I spoke Spanish to them, they gave me a chance to explain that I hadn't taken any pictures yet, and they let me put my Olympus away in my backpack.

The following day Sandra and I found a little hotel in the jungle near Palenque, where toucans clacked and howler monkeys screeched in welcome. The next morning we descended many steep steps, deep into the Temple of the Inscriptions, to marvel at the hidden crypt of King Pa'kal. A few days later a wonderful *trio romántico* sang just for us in a restaurant's courtyard in Mérida, beneath a huge rubber tree.

Along the road we stopped to buy bunches of bananas wherever we saw them growing. The farmer would hack through the thick stem with a *machete*, his youngsters staring at us from behind their mother's skirt. One roadside fruit stand had a wooden press, like a garlic press but sized to fit a whole pineapple. The vendor placed an empty pitcher on the ground beneath a sturdy screened frame—then he put an uncut pineapple on the screen and slammed the handle of the wooden top panel down onto it—Wham! The freshest pineapple juice in the universe streamed into the pitcher; then it was poured into glasses and served to us with a smile.

Ahh, and the mangos! After a time you begin to recognize the mango trees from a distance. In a land of tropical vegetation that leans or slumps every which way, the trunk of a mango is straight, and its branches form a broad blimp of a canopy. The long grooved leaves are like those of a peach tree, but darker green, thick and waxy. In every town we drove through, mango trees were hung with dangling ripe fruit. Some were rounded, red and gold, others yellow ovals.

There were the immense red-and-green mangos too, long as eggplants. We bought them at roadside stands for the equivalent of a nickel each. One vendor enjoyed telling us how to eat them: "First, you take all your clothes off. Then you sit on the edge of a bathtub. You hold the mango with a fork through the bottom, and you peel it with a short, sharp knife. A mango as big as this one, it's best if you share it with a friend."

One afternoon at a motel near Chichén Itzá, red-and-gold mangos littered the parking lot while orange orioles feasted. "They're five centavos each," the manager told us, "but many of them are *pasados* already—ah, *¡lleva los que quieres!* Take as many as you want!"

We pulled a pillowcase out of the camping gear and stuffed it with our new favorite fruits. And so, full of mangos and high spirits, the green semiautomatic rolled into Cancún.

6 El Diablo y El Aristófanes

Sandra and I spent our first day in Cancún applying Coppertone #4 to each other's backs and turning golden tan on the beach of Hotel Camino Real, open only one month. Its sleek expanse harmonized with the cream-colored rocks of Punta Cancún, the spot from which my friends and I had plunged into those turquoise whitecaps back in 1972. This time the sea was calm; we floated on aquamarine wavelets, snorkeled around the reef at the point and snacked sumptuously at the hotel's outdoor grill.

Nearly six weeks had elapsed since our departure from New York. Most nights on the road we had found inexpensive hotel rooms or places to pitch our tent, but in Cancún we were told that all five spanking-new hotels were charging at least one hundred dollars per night. A lifeguard invited us to hang our hammocks inside his wooden lifeguard's tower at Playa Chac Mool. He even gave us a mosquito coil to light and set on the sandy floor. It would keep us from being eaten alive during the night—or so he said!

The next afternoon an attractive guy we met on the beach stopped mid-sentence to stare at the bites on Sandra's long legs. He knew of a campground at Punta Sam where we could pitch our tent, he told us. That's where we were headed, when something extraordinary caught my eye.

In the arms of a young man in a cowboy hat seated by the passenger window of a parked VW, something tawny and spotted stretched its head toward me. Then it tucked under the man's arm again.

Whatever it was, it had captured me. I found myself beside the car. "It's my ocelot, Pepe," the handsome fellow confided, scratching the fur between the animal's rounded ears. Its clear golden eyes sized me up—too big for prey. Now the creature sank its claws into the upholstered seat and stretched again. The way the muscles slid under its patterned hide was entrancing.

The man stretched out his own muscular paw, similar in color to the ocelot's. "They call me," he said in deep tones, "El Diablo," and we shook hands—his was quite warm. "I'm waiting for a friend, and then we're going for tacos—why don't you and your friend join us? I know a good place—do you like chile?"

So Diablo was already up to tricks. His question, *"¿Te gusta el chile?"* was a double-entendre that I then understood only as a reference to a Mexican chili pepper. How was I to know the word also was used for a part of the male anatomy? Any response a woman might make would be good for a laugh. Now I know how to foil a joker asking this question: answer: *"Sí, me gusta el picante,"* (Yes, I like spicy food). Then *el pícaro* (the rogue) will know you're onto him.

Diablo turned out to be a terrific friend, always in good humor, although so much of it was saucy. He and the other fellow worked for FONATUR, the federal agency that was creating the infrastructure for the new tourist resort—roads, the airport, water, electrical and communications systems. Their connections soon had me teaching English to engineers, architects and *políticos* there.

Now is the time I must mention a certain contretemps that Sandra and I experienced earlier, back in Mexico City, regarding the transmission of the green semi. The day after my birthday party at Paco's place, Sandra and I drove to la Zona Rosa, a downtown area akin to Greenwich Village or North Beach or parts of Cambridge, touristy, but hip, too. I parked the semi at a lot, and *el encargado* asked me to leave the key. I told him I couldn't, because my car was different from other VWs and was sure to give him problems.

"No, ningún problema," he insisted, staring at the unusual dashboard.

When we returned hours later, the semiautomatic was parked obstructing other cars, with its wheels turned sharply to the left, and the key in the ignition; when I tried to get it into gear, it groaned but refused to move. I sat still at the wheel a moment, feeling nauseated.

The *encargado* tried to tell me that the car was going dead when we drove in; I turned my back on him.

Sandra and I walked across the street into the lobby of the Hotel Geneva to call Paco and tell him about the fix we were in. But we didn't know how to use a Mexican pay phone yet. How lucky we were that a skinny guy with a big smile, dressed in a sports jacket and powder-blue turtleneck, was standing near, offering the right coin for the pay phone and demonstrating how to use it. He overheard the tale of the semi as I related it to Paco. When I hung up, this fellow nearly exploded with the serendipity of it all—it just so happened that he was *muy amigos* with Helmut or Horst or teutonic Tomi, the head honcho at the biggest VW agency in Mexico City.

His own name, he told us with a little bow, was Aristófanes Ramirez, and he desired nothing more than to help us through our difficulties. Helmut-Horst sent a tow truck for our comatose vehicle, and several days later the semi was ready to go, for a considerable sum of money. But the parking lot paid most of it, after Aristófanes worked them over verbally. I was impressed and amused with his highfalutin' ways. I invited him to join us on our journey, since the career in photojournalism he mentioned didn't seem to give him much to do but rescue damsels in distress.

"I'd be delighted to meet you ladies at some later point in your journey," he answered. The wide smile in his narrow face looked a bit reptilian. Unfortunately, he said, he had pressing engagements at the moment. Something about him reminded me of Diego Rivera's renderings of Cortés—sallow and chinless, slim but with a protruding belly. I thought Aristófanes might be gay. Before leaving D.F., I introduced him to Paco, who waved every warning flag he owned in my face. I attributed Paco's angst about the guy to class snobbery, and decided to forget about it.

Now, back to cowboy-hatted Diablo on that second afternoon in Cancún: over tacos at La Parrilla, a little joint no wider than my arm span, I could see Sandra and Diablo getting hotter than the salsa. Diablo's friend was very attractive too, but I realized from a conversation I overheard between the men that there was a woman, a Dutch woman, waiting for the friend at home. Still, they were brainstorming about work for me through FONATUR, and each idea sounded better than the last.

That night Sandra and I set up our tent at the campground. The next day while she hung out with Diablo, I visited each of Cancún's five hotels. Starting at Hotel Bojorquez, the smallest one, I showed the personnel managers my résumé and told them my plans for English lessons for their employees. I should say I sold them my plans—all five agreed to hire me at the rate I had dared to suggest, twenty-five dollars per hour. I could start as soon as I had working papers, all five cautioned.

Aristófanes had confided that one of his bosom buddies was a high mucky-muck in the immigration department. I called Ari to tell him about these great work offers—*"¡Qué maravilla!"* he congratulated me. He'd be only too delighted, etc. It might cost a bit of money, however. For now, just mail him my visa special delivery, get letters from the hotels offering me jobs, and he'd take care of everything else, he said.

When that was done, I fell to finding an apartment. Then I bought a folding table, chairs and some pots and pans, and learned my way around the dusty hamlet/construction camp that was Cancún. Sandra spent a few days and nights with her dear Diablo. Then she tore herself away—she flew back to New York to look for a job.

I began teaching a lunch-hour class to young engineers and architects at FONATUR. I told the human resources administrator that my papers were *"en trámite"* in Mexico City, a phrase Aristófanes had used. Once I had learned that phrase, I started hearing it everywhere—a utility contract, a bank account, anything you might want to do once you were no longer a tourist required a *trámite*, that is, papers in triplicate, lots of seals, geologic periods of time…and money.

The FONATUR job led to classes at the airport, with the firemen, administration and maintenance staff. One or two afternoons weekly I taught waiters and kitchen staff at Mauna Loa Restaurant in the hotel zone, which would turn into Discoteca Krakatoa every night. I greeted the kitchen staff in Chinese that I had learned from my NYC students, and the delighted chef made shrimp in lobster sauce just for me. Also I got started at a public kindergarten on Avenue Yaxchilán. Everywhere, employers asked to see my papers, and everywhere I said they were *"en trámite."*

But I started worrying that the six-month visa issued in July, which I had mailed off to Aristófanes, was running out. I called Ari's house and spoke to his mother—she didn't know when she'd see him, she said. I wrote and called several more times, from public phone offices, of course. I got a P.O. box and mailed him the address. I called again, and finally I caught him in another of his moments of extreme serendipity: his *cuate* in immigration, a friend so close you could call him a twin, had at last been able to secure the signature of an even higher mucky-muck, one who was about to ascend to the *very highest ranks*. So it was the greatest good fortune that Aristófanes' friend had reached him before he left the immigration service. And YES! The High Honcho had agreed to authorize my change of immigration status from tourist to FM3.

Now if I would simply wire Aristófanes four hundred dollars, he would have those papers ready for me in a *"dos-por-tres!"* He itemized: two hundred and fifty for the signature, and one-hundred and fifty for special rapid expedition of the papers.

Where was this money to come from, you may be asking yourself. I did have some income from those classes I mentioned every week. But my savings from teaching in NYC had run out some time ago. Still, I had another resource I could count on. Before Uncle Arturo died, he had created a trust fund to be split nine ways, and I was one of the recipients. So I called the bank in New York and had four hundred dollars wired to Sr. A. Ramirez.

Aristófanes arrived at the Cancún airport a few days later with the air of one descending from Mount Olympus. Here it was, the signature of his *amigo importantísimo* on a lengthy form. It even had a red seal that was smudged, but of course it was the seal of the *Secretaría de Relaciones Exteriores*.

"Isn't this *fantástico*?" Aristófanes demanded rhetorically. "Do you know how *hard* it is to obtain the signature of such a significant figure in the Federal Government, and just before the offices shut down for the entire month of December. All that's needed now," Aristófanes showed me, "is for you to fill in the personal information here, and sign these two forms, and I shall have the completed documents sent to you by courier service, next week!"

So the papers weren't finished after all. In that case why hadn't he simply mailed these for me to sign and mail back to him, I asked, feeling very uneasy.

"Oh, but Déborah, it's the end of *noviembre*! There was no time for mail! This is *urgente*!" Of course.

"Meanwhile," he said, "I'd like to treat you to a weekend in Cozumel, the kind of weekend you deserve after working so hard this fall." Aristófanes was very close with the manager of a great hotel there, where he could get us a suite for the price of a regular room.

"We're ordering champagne," he said at the hotel restaurant, his elbows firmly planted on the white tablecloth, "to celebrate your new FM3 status, with permission to live and work in Mexico!"

"*¡Salud! ¡Suerte! ¡Chin-chin!*" we toasted each other many times over.

And gay? Did you agree with me when I was speculating that Aristófanes might be gay? If only....

On Monday I drove Aristófanes to the airport for his return trip to Mexico City. In the lobby, just as he was waving *adiós*, an immigration officer asked to see my passport. He stared at my photo and asked me to accompany him to the office of the *comandante* of the airport.

From behind his heavy desk, the even heavier *comandante* scanned the passport and scanned me. Then he asked, "With what legal authorization are you teaching English at the airport?"

"Oh," I responded with confidence, "my papers are *en trámite* in Mexico City. In fact, I already have the signature of H. Mucky Muck. My friend has promised that my FM3 will be sent to me by courier service this very week."

"*¿De veras?*" el comandante asked without a blink. "Then how is it possible that I have your passport in my hands? The *Secretaría de Relaciones Exteriores* in Mexico City must have your passport in order to *tramitar* working papers."

Have you heard of *El Sumidero*, the deepest canyon in Mexico, thousands of feet deeper than the Grand Canyon? Into *El Sumidero* my heart descended, as understanding of Aristófanes' deceit came upon me. My hands and my knees trembled, there in the chair in front of the *el comandante*, and I had to grasp the armrests. That *hijo de su madre* Aristófanes.

For a long while I had no answer for the *comandante*. Meanwhile, his stare did not let up. Finally I regained control of my power of speech. Quietly I said that I had believed that my papers were *en trámite*, but now I would start the process all over.

Diablo and I had joked about this *comandante* several times: He was an old stone face of a man, and his two last names were easy to pun with. By changing just one letter in each name, the Spanish meaning would be "Big Dirty Old Thing." So at this moment, with my morale on the floor and my nerves cavorting on the ceiling, I mispronounced his name. I said to the *comandante* something like:

"Por favor, *Señor* Big Dirty Old Thing, please give me back my passport."

His pockmarked cheeks turned red. His ears and his nose, too. There was no question but that he had heard this pun before, maybe repeatedly, possibly since childhood. He let out a long hiss.

Finally *el comandante* spoke from between his teeth. "Here. Your passport. You have twenty-four hours to leave the country."

Silently I took the passport and walked out of his office *cabisbaja*, a single word that means "with my head held low." I found my car in the parking lot and drove the fifteen kilometers back to Cancún. Diablo's place was where I headed. At his door I asked him to help me pack. He tucked his ocelot, Pepe, under his arm and got in the car with me. First we bought some beer, then we drove around the market looking for boxes.

Back in my one-room apartment, we quietly began packing every item I owned. Pepe seemed to appreciate the mood in the small room; he stayed close to me, rubbing his smooth, spotted sides against my bare legs. Diablo and I started the job in gloomy silence, but little by little we got back to our customary banter. The huge tortoise skull Diablo and I had once found on the beach wouldn't fit in my bags, so I placed it on top of a box to leave it for him.

Once we finished the packing, Diablo and I sat on boxes, talking in low tones, playing with Pepe and staring at the tortoise skull. Sometime around midnight I heard myself say, *"Yo tengo la cabeza más dura que esa tortuga.* My head is harder than that *tortuga's.* If they want me to leave, they can come and get me."

Diablo proposed a toast: *"Aquí estamos, y aquí nos quedamos."* Here we are, and here we will remain. We drank a couple of beers on it, and that was that.

 # A Surprise in the Kindergarten Classroom

My first winter in Cancún, besides teaching at the airport, at the restaurant-disco Mauna Loa and at FONATUR, the agency in charge of Cancún's infrastructure, I also taught after-school classes at a kindergarten on the edge of Palapas Park. No more than twenty *niñitos* were in the group, but every one was jumpy as a grasshopper at the end of the school day, when I arrived.

I taught the kids "Head and Shoulders, Knees and Toes." One afternoon I made the mistake of getting down on my hands and knees with them, encouraging each to choose a red wooden Cuisenaire learning rod and then a yellow one; in no time, those rods were flying! Pablo had snatched Amanda's rod and she was pitching reds, blues and yellows at him. Monica's little white rod got lodged in her nose.

I had never taught kindergarten before, nor had I had training for working with little ones, but soon I found that they would do what I wanted if I led them in songs like "One-Two, Buckle my Shoe," "Old MacDonald" and "Ten Little Indians." We were hopping to "The Hokey Pokey" one afternoon when a Telemundo TV Network van with antennae and dishes on the roof pulled up alongside the classroom.

Everyone was used to seeing TV and film companies in Cancún, even though we still had no TV service. Much later, when service finally began, I discovered that many *telenovelas* (Latino soap operas) featured bronzed divers pursuing rascals under the crystalline waters of Cancún, Isla Mujeres or Cozumel.

But the TV news, like the newspapers, adored bizarre anomalies: middle-class homes with anteaters for pets, churches open on three sides to the jungle. A news story about an English class in a public kindergarten would be just one more bit of human-interest exotica.

That's what I thought when the principal of the school burst into the room with a media person, an urbane young man with a clipboard and a worried brow. "Don't stop what you're doing!" the principal waved her arms at me. I looked at her in surprise; no one had asked us to stop what we were doing.

So we put our right feet in and our left hands out while a crowd gathered in the doorway. After a few moments, the crowd parted and a pale character shiny with sweat slunk in. The hair encircling his bald head looked stringy, oily. I must be exaggerating here…or am I? He certainly didn't walk in like a VIP—his steps were irregular, as if he weren't sure where he was going.

He reminded me of someone, perhaps one of Diego Rivera's portrayals of the Spanish conquistadores—potbelly over spindly legs, chinless face with five-o'clock shadow, furtive eyes. Oh, now I knew! He reminded me of Aristófanes! But this one seemed to be afraid of something, maybe of the children. He didn't greet them, nor did he greet me. But I did recognize him.

He was Luis Echeverría, the president of Mexico. It was his government that had ordered the development of Cancún, Mexico's first officially designed tourist resort. When a commission had chosen Cancún as the most favorable beach in all of Mexico's 25,000 miles of coastline, I don't believe their study mentioned that the family of Echeverría's wife owned the land, and that it could be leased to hotel consortiums at rates humbling those of all other seashore real estate.

Anyway, here before me was the president of Mexico, his thin yellowish *guayabera* shirt sticking to his sweating torso, watching my kiddos and me do the hokey pokey. Did protocol demand that I greet him first? Should I invite him to join us?

But he beat me to the punch. *"¿Eres voluntaria en esta clase?"* he asked sharply. "Are you a volunteer teacher here?"

Not *"Buenas tardes."* Not *"Hola, niños, ¿cómo están?"* Not a left foot or even a finger into the circle.

"Are you a volunteer president?" I wanted to ask in response. Was I a volunteer? Well, they weren't paying me much. It occurred to me that he might bust me for playing illegal hokey pokey with minors. But I just answered, "No," and hokey pokied on. By the time my right foot was out, so was Echeverría, and the crowd had turned their backs to us. One Telemundo van after another drove away. Teaching English in Cancún? That's what it's all about!

8 I Find the Name of the School

Uncle Arturo had given me a little book called *The World of the Mayas,* written for schoolchildren by Victor Von Hagen. The illustrations were cartoon versions of Mayan *bas reliefs* and glyphs I remembered seeing when Sandra and I visited Palenque, Chichén Itzá and Tulúm. In this slim paperback, a complex and grand civilization was compressed into fewer than two hundred pages, double-spaced. I had read parts to Sandra as we approached Mérida and at our hotel near Chichén Itzá. Now that I was living in Cancún, I spent one sweltering afternoon in my hammock, finishing the book.

In the appendix I came upon a map of the Mayan region with an unusual place name, a word that didn't sound like Cancún or Tulúm or Xelha. On an island in the Laguna de Términos, in the Gulf of Mexico, an ancient city called Xicalango perched on the border between the Mayan and Aztec realms. On one side people spoke Mayan—on the other side, Nahuatl. Xicalango was Nahuatl for "the place where the language changes."

"¡Perfecto!" I exclaimed, and stood up out of my hammock. Unable to keep my discovery to myself, I slipped on my flip-flops, locked my door and skipped across Avenue Tulúm to the home of my friend Isabel.

At that time it was hardly necessary to look both ways before crossing Cancún's main drag; there weren't more than one thousand cars and trucks circulating in the whole town. Besides that, Avenue Tulúm was being paved and repaved every time you crossed the street. The same was true for Bulevard Kukulkán, the road to the hotel zone. People spoke of road construction companies with perpetual contracts. In any case, I couldn't run across; what with work crews and mounds of sand, Avenue Tulúm was more like an obstacle course than a racetrack back then.

At Doña Isabel's, a slim Mayan woman in a spanking-white *huipil* opened the door, bade me sit down at the gleaming dining table, and went to tell her employer that she had a visitor. An excited visitor, she might have added.

"Escuela Xicalango!" echoed Isabel when I told her my idea. "What a wonderful name for a language school. Yes, let's make a language school," she nodded, her eyes bright.

Isabel was *toda una dama*, a lady of leisure, the wife of a state official. I had met her on the tennis court, and we had had a number of conversations, some decent games and a few *limonadas* together. Her English was quite good and her personality was charming, but her credentials as a potential partner were fantastic. Did I know anything about starting a business in Mexico? Could I meet the legal requirements for opening a school? With Isabel as a partner, I would have experience and position on my side—what a coup that would be.

Isabel and I sat in the shuttered shade of her dining room under the silent ceiling fan, discussing possible sites for the school as we drank coffee served us by the Mayan maid. My cup and saucer made distinct reflections on the glossy dark wood of the dining room set—unlike my furniture, the table was absolutely free of dust. This was striking in the Cancún of 1975, when every other building was under construction.

I commented on this remarkable cleanliness. "Yes," Isabel responded, tapping her manicured nails on the mahogany, "this María keeps the place clean, but I get tired of her at times. I tell her what to do, and she does something else entirely." The diminutive woman brought us fresh *pan dulce*, shell-shaped ones called conchas and the ones like ears, *orejas*, and smiled warmly at me. Her face reminded me of fine engravings on the temple walls in Palenque. "Would you like milk with your coffee, Doña Deborah?" she asked me.

"How did you know?" I smiled back.

"My name is Socorro," the woman introduced herself gently, adding the milk. Small as she was, she gave a formidable impression, with her erect posture and her confident gaze. "Please let me know if there is anything else I can do for you," she added before moving away toward the kitchen.

"María!" Isabel called her back again. "Bring the dust pan! You've dropped crumbs on the floor."

It seemed more likely that I had dropped the crumbs. And why was Isabel calling the woman "María?"

I love when you muse in silence about something, and then someone answers your unspoken question.

"I call them all María," Isabel confided. "It's hard to keep their names straight. And they're all the same."

"Hmmm," I thought. "All the same?" This should have been enough to put me off. But I was invested in the idea of Isabel as a partner.

Shortly after the idea of the school was born, I returned to New York to pack up my Park Slope apartment and parcel out my furniture and other belongings. My secondhand Persian lamb coat went to one friend, my high boots from Tío Arturo to another. When would I ever need winter clothes again? While I was taping closed a box of books, the phone rang. It was a personnel manager at New York City Board of Education, offering me an appointment, a full-time ESL teaching position at Clara Barton High School, a Brooklyn high school for girls. I had left New York because I hadn't been able to find such a position. But I had already made my choice: to give life a go in Mexico.

Sim, the son of Sylvia and Rahim, had bet me a cheeseburger at the Riviera in Sheridan Square that I wasn't going back to Cancún—I said I'd be out of NY and on the road by November 15th. On the 14th, when I met him to claim my burger, a dozen of my friends had assembled for a surprise send-off, toasting me with jibes and good wishes. I felt like the chili on the cheeseburger, hot, tangy and delicious.

When I got back to Cancún, Doña Isabel was off in Mexico City. She was doleful when she reappeared. Her grandchildren needed her, she said with resignation. She simply couldn't commit to being a partner in a school because she would need to return to Mexico City often.

"I'm so sorry," she said. She'd be glad to help me when she could. But she would be away again the rest of the month.

"Please feel free," Isabel said, "to come by when I get back, and I'll see how I can be of help. Especially once the school is up and running…"

Maybe she had thought I wouldn't come back from New York. Or maybe she had thought, "Those Debbys, they're all the same!"

So I was on my own. But at the least, I had the right name for the school—Escuela Xicalango, the Place Where the Language Changes.

 *9*   *Becoming Déborah*

Cancún, variously translated from Mayan as "Pot of Gold at the End of the Rainbow" and as "Nest of Vipers." How did a Jewish girl raised in Brooklyn and Long Island become *una pionera de Cancún*, while her New York friends were still asking each other, "Debby's moving to *Can-WHAT*?"

One afternoon in 2010 I received in the mail a key to this mystery. In a box with other things that had belonged to my Uncle Arturo I found a crumbling copy of a Spanish magazine called *"Blanco y Negro."* On its cover was an imperial shield with two phoenixes; the title arched over the page in ornate crimson letters. Inside the magazine I discovered a fountain-penned inscription:

March 21st, 1929. Presented to Arthur Weiss, who obtained
first place in the Spanish match held to-day.

—*J. Leo Pasternak*

My uncle Arthur was fifteen in 1929, a sophomore at DeWitt
Clinton High School in the Bronx. Spanish so suited him that my
mother and most of the family took to calling him "Arturo,"
adding continental flair to *seders* and *sukkahs* ever after.

Arturo's little sister, my mother Leonora, called Lee, was a
high-school whiz at French, but she didn't begin to *hablar español*
until twenty-five years later. Once my parents began traveling in
Latin America with Arturo and his wife Eileen, Spanish words *cha-
cha*'d their way into Mom's vocabulary, and from hers into mine.
My father, Irving, an editor and PR man, began arranging
promotional trips to Acapulco and Taxco for his company's sales
force, always during the winter months. I couldn't be absent from
my high school classes for weeks at a time, so I got to stay at my
best friend's house. But each enthusiastic post card, each abalone
bangle bracelet, each of my father's slides of young men in
swimsuits diving nonchalantly off tall cliffs intrigued me more.

Soon I was attending City College in New York, and Lee, my
mom, switched to part-time at her editorial job, in order to become
an ACE student, in Adult Continuing Education, at Queens
College. She matriculated at the age of forty-seven. Her hair was
long and blonde; now that she was a co-ed, she let loose her
French twist, and her blonde ponytail fell in waves down her back.
She got her ears pierced, too. My father ribbed her, calling her "a
straight B student," but it was only a joke—she got almost all A's.

My mom and I sometimes did our college Spanish homework
together at the kitchen table, snacking on guacamole and chips.
Nobody else in Plainview, Long Island, had tasted guacamole yet.
And *ceviche*? It became my favorite food, although my friends
turned it down: "Raw fish? Ewww!"

By fifty Lee had her BA and her acceptance to the City
University doctoral program in cultural anthropology. "Do you
think I should study Tongan?" she mused. "I don't know. Because
maybe I'll want to do my field study with the Kwaquiutl."

That fall I was a senior at City College, an English major, and the college found me a volunteer position teaching ESL to adults in an office across the street from the UN. Most of my students were Cuban immigrants, like the lady lawyer who spent her days operating an elevator and the economics professor with the janitorial position. After class I drank sweet dark coffee from cups like thimbles with my students, trying to make sense of the machine-gun Spanish spraying from their lips. I was enthralled…with the students, the language and the job.

But the winter of 1970 held no festive holiday season for my family. The week before Christmas, near the end of Lee's first graduate semester, while she was painting the front door red to welcome my brother home from the service, her legs buckled under her. She was diagnosed with acute myeloid leukemia.

For the previous fourteen years Lee had worked with microbiologists, so she knew where the most advanced cancer care could be had—at Sloan-Kettering Memorial Hospital in Manhattan.

Lee was the editor of the annual symposium book at Cold Spring Harbor Laboratory of Quantitative Biology. The director of the lab was Dr. James Watson, Nobel Prize laureate, along with Dr. Francis Crick, for the discovery of the structure of the DNA molecule. On a hospital visit to her, Dr. Watson comforted my mother with science: "The research we're doing now is going to lead to effective treatments for this disease," he said gently. He was right, and it did comfort her to hear him say it. But it didn't save her.

While Lee was in the hospital I visited daily, often with Moses, my best friend from City College. When Lee and I ran out of talk, Moses filled in with his sardonic take on the fiscal crisis, the Vietnam War or the price of tomatoes. Good-looking, bright and affectionate toward both Lee and me, Moses was Romanian, like my mom's parents. Moses was born in Bucharest in 1947, and had learned Yiddish first, then Hebrew when his family reached Israel in 1949, then English when they came to New York in 1960. The accent that went with that first language was a comical surprise, coming from the mouth of this tall, blond youth dressed in khakis and loafers, like the yachtsmen he emulated.

Sometimes Moses and I would enter my mom's hospital room to find a Puerto Rican or Dominican patient hooked up to a drip stand and deep in Spanish conversation with Lee. Or a whole Latino family would be standing around Lee's bed, leaning in to hear her halting explanation of what the doctor had said to them. On other occasions a nurse might be with her, taking notes on the questions of a patient's family. I chimed in as an interpreter, and so did my Uncle Arturo.

Arturo was a regular at the hospital, too. He had already done such service for his wife, my aunt Eileen, during her cancer treatments two or three years earlier. Her treatment went on interminably, but it hadn't done the trick.

I visited my mother every day she was at the hospital, and I heard her comment on it to Uncle Arturo. The next time he and I were leaving the hospital together, he slipped three fifty-dollar bills into my coat pocket, and said, "Go buy yourself some boots." The ones I chose were smooth caramel-colored leather up to my knees, with straps around the ankles and little golden buckles. I was wild about my boots, and about my uncle.

Early on in her hospital stays, Lee asked me to attend one of her graduate seminars in the new City University Center on 42nd Street, a thrill for an undergraduate like me. Afterwards, I took the bus straight to Sloan-Kettering to tell her about it, and found Lee asleep post-chemo, her face the color of ashes. I don't know what happened to me when I saw her, but a nurse had to pick me up off the floor.

I was twenty-four and had not yet finished the first semester of my NYU master's program. The day before Christmas, Lee gave me enough money to buy an Indian silk scarf for each nurse on her floor. Early Christmas morning, the red-on-pink and blue-on-magenta paisley scarves floated from my bag as I exited the elevator. The nursing station went silent.

The nurses must have realized at once that I hadn't heard yet. Their pleasant faces now turned so somber told me the story: Lee was gone.

At her funeral, our friend Latif spoke with eloquence about Lee's gifts for friendship, insight and good humor. More than one hundred people embraced me, and I vaguely remember holding my arms stiff at my sides; I couldn't even hug back.

At six on the dot for a week, family and friends arrived to sit *shiva* in the living room, to drink coffee and eat pastries they brought in pink bakery boxes. I looked at their behavior with the detachment of an anthropologist. The friends and relatives wanted to hear my plans for the future, but by then I had made up my mind to think about only one thing: MEXICO!

Two months later, in February of 1972, a lawyer read Lee's will aloud. She had left me $900—enough to pay for months south of the border. I located a Spanish language program in Guadalajara, and *¡Adiós, New York!*

10 In Cancún: Assessing the Competition

All through the fall of 1975, great lengths of red tape were unwinding from one spool and rewinding on another, and finally the FM3 temporary working papers were delivered. Now I began teaching in the five hotels that had initially given me the go-ahead, and I continued with some FONATUR classes.

But personnel turnover created a problem for the hotels and consequently a problem for me. New hotels opened every few days. I started teaching in November of 1975; by March the number of hotels in the zona hotelera had doubled or tripled. Wherever a department chief was unpopular, an entire department might pick up and move to a new hotel down the road. Often before a hotel opened, its administration would fix the salary scale a trifle above the going rate, and hire a complete staff in a day or two.

Naturally, human resource people were not keen on English training for staff they knew to be as ephemeral as butterflies. Personnel managers were working overtime, trying to keep the restaurants and registration desks functioning; they refused to worry about ESL. Classes couldn't progress with such turbulence. Twenty students might show up on Monday, two on Wednesday, and fourteen new ones on Friday.

Aside from that, I didn't enjoy teaching students who were paid to attend classes. They came late. They forgot their materials. They forgot everything from one lesson to the next. This wasn't much better than teaching squirmy middle-school kids in Queens.

At the same time, people I knew were begging for private classes. They offered to gather groups for me that would meet in their homes, in a park, in an evangelical church.

"Debes de poner una escuela," people told me all day long. "You should open a school."

"But there is an English language school already," Diablo told me. "It's next to *Mercado 23*," one of the two large outdoor markets. I thought I had better visit it. Maybe it would be best for me to get a job there.

'23' meant that the market was part of Residential Block 23 *(Manzana 23)*, among the first neighborhoods built in Cancún. It encompassed four or five hundred nearly identical cinderblock houses, a primary school, and two or three churches, on curving streets surrounding the market. The roofs were flat, with PVC pipes protruding for rainwater runoff.

Assuming that homeowners would want to add a second floor later, builders left eight or ten feet of rebar sticking straight up on the four corners of each house. To protect the rebar against rust, overturned coke bottles topped each metallic shoot. Where second stories were already under construction, scaffolding made of mottled sticks from the jungle surrounded the houses. Out front there might be some *flamboyán* trees, graceful branches covered with red blossoms, or some pines or a coconut palm, all rather short—everything had been planted no more than four years earlier.

The only exceptions were the tall *chicozapote* trees, with nubbly gray bark and deep hatch marks slashed into the trunk with machetes. Whenever possible, builders left those trees standing; they were still producing *chicle*, the chewing gum Mayans had favored for centuries.

Across the parking lot from the market, I saw a handwritten sign taped to the window of a narrow storefront. It announced *"Clases de Inglés, ¡INSCRIPCIONES ABIERTAS!"* (Enrolling Now!). Graffiti-scarred wooden desks, the heavy, torturous ones with the chairs attached, were arranged in two rows with a wide aisle between them, facing a huge teacher's desk at the end of the room. Had everything come from some tumbledown public school? On the wall behind the teacher's "pulpit" hung a dusty blackboard with *"página 29"* scribbled on it. The two students in the room were seated one on the right and one on the left, the girl a few rows ahead of the boy. Even in that small room, the students were so far apart that practice or conversation between them would have been impossible.

I'd never have them sit like that, I said to myself.

My master's program in ESL at NYU was supposed to include six months of student teaching in a master teacher's classroom. The faculty member assigned to set up this arrangement had died before completing it, and no one followed up, so I had no supervised student teaching. But one day a master teacher had come to my Queens middle school classroom. Few if any of the kids were paying attention to my lesson. Ms. Master Teacher changed the atmosphere immediately by asking the kids to help her push their desks into a circle. From that day on I did my best to arrange my classrooms for student-to-student communication, for every grade and every level.

And I'm going to see to it that my students have better books than those, I sniffed, noticing the copies of *Inglés sin Maestro*, or "English Without a Teacher," on the students' desks. I'd thumbed through this bestseller; according to this text, the English word for "blender" was "liquidor." The illustrations seemed to be from the 'forties, and the book featured dialogs with teachers saying things like "Open immediately your copybooks."

The three people in the room eyed me curiously.

"¿Puedo ayudarle?" (Can I help you?) the smiling young man nearly hidden behind the big desk asked. He was a slim *yucateco*, obvious from the breadth of his face. When you see someone who looks Mexican, but whose head appears wider than it is long, that person is probably a Mayan, a *yucateco* Mayan.

"I see you're teaching English here," I said, addressing him in English. I felt flustered by the rush of negative impressions I'd gotten in my first minute in the "school." Brilliant, I chided myself, inwardly, is this how you plan to make a friend here?

"It seems everybody in Cancún wants to learn English," I started again, hopeful of starting a conversation. The teacher nodded his head yes, but also bobbed it from side to side. What was he unsure of?

Okay, let me be more concrete this time, I resolved. "How many students do you teach here in this school?" I asked Mr. Teacher.

"Oiga," the young man responded in the polite form, smiling more warmly than ever, "usted habla español, *¿verdad?"* (You speak Spanish, right?)

"Sí, hablo español," I answered.

"Bueno, pues," (Well, then) he replied, and continued in Spanish, "why don't you ask me in Spanish?"

I was floored. *"Inglés sin Maestro"* was right. I did as he requested and asked my question in Spanish. He told me that he and the owner of the school had about 125 students learning English. He told me this in Spanish.

Yes, I decided, I *will* start my own school.

Making a Home for Escuela Xicalango

Doña Isabel de Político, the woman who three months earlier had exclaimed, "Debby! Let's start a school!" wasn't going to help until the school opened, if then. But it wasn't long before I met Domingo, an interesting-looking blue-eyed *yucateco* who had gone to high school in upstate New York—his English was perfect, and he had always wanted to start a school, he said.

I pointed out to Domingo a one-story brick house that I had come across, a pleasant-looking place in spite of the tangle of thorny weeds in the front yard. The location couldn't have been better for a school for adults: it sat on the curve where Avenue Uxmal meets Avenue Nader, one block east of Avenue Tulúm. All the buses passed nearby, and it was equidistant between the hotel zone and *la colonia*, the sprawling working-class neighborhood where most of our potential students lived. Domingo liked the house too, but when we peeked in the louvered windows we found that some construction workers were using it as a dormitory.

"Let's come back very early tomorrow," I suggested. Around six the next morning I arrived at the brick house before the men left for work. Domingo was a no-show, but I was serious about finding out who owned the place.

They had built this house, one worker said, but no one wanted to tell me more—I got the feeling they were camping there rent-free. Three different men answered my questions with *"No sé,"* in the Yucatán style, letting their sing-song tones drop between the first and second words. I think the barrel-chested *jefe* of the group must have felt too embarrassed to repeat the same phrase.

"It is *very* complicated," he told me. His crew had built the house for a couple that had since divorced. "Who is the owner now?" he asked the heavens, turning his palms toward the sky. But with more insistence on my part, finally he gave me the name of the wife, and on a second early morning visit, he relinquished her phone number. She lived four hours south, in Chetumal.

The only place to make calls was a public phone office, where one took a number and waited until a booth became free. After several calls I managed to get in touch with the owner; a few more convinced her to talk about renting the place. At last Doña arrived in Cancún, and over coffee and cake we negotiated a rental contract for one year. Domingo didn't show for this meeting either, nor did he come up with his share of the down payment for the tables, chairs and blackboard. But every time I walked on Avenue Tulúm, someone else would stop me to ask whether I was the *la maestra de inglés,* and when courses would begin. There was no backpedaling for me.

So I prepared to move out of my studio apartment in Supermanzana 5, and into the two-bedroom house that was to become Escuela Xicalango. Diablo volunteered to help me move. It must have been a Sunday; when we pulled up in front of the house with all my things, the workers were still asleep in their hammocks. We returned to the car and slammed the doors as loudly as possible. At last the *jefe* staggered out, rubbing his eyes. He looked at Doña's rental agreement in disbelief, but finally he agreed they'd all be out that evening.

Months before, while Sandra was still in Cancún, Diablo had invited the two of us to stay at his little house. Sandra would stay in Diablo's room, but I needed my own hammock. I could hang it on metal hooks set into the walls in the living room, so Diablo took us hammock shopping.

Doña Nancy was standing, her broad back to us, weaving a gorgeous hammock on the front porch of her house when we approached. Weavers use a tall wooden frame, its separate legs connected with a trestle about six feet long. They weave their cotton or nylon threads back and forth across the warp with a wooden shuttle.

Diablo called out, *"¡Hola, Doña Nancy!"* and she turned to face us. Instantly a sly grin lit her face.

"¡Mare, lindo!" she said to Diablo, "you lucky guy! I've just finished weaving the most beautiful hammock for three!"

I learned to love sleeping in that hammock. You lie down in it on a diagonal, pulling one edge over your head; once you're settled in it, the hammock swings and hugs you to sleep. There is no bed as comfortable for a hot climate, and if your friend is sleeping with someone next door, well, in a colorful hammock you don't feel so alone.

As soon as Sandra left, my hammock and I moved into a studio apartment near Parque las Palapas. It was about six months later that I got the lease for the brick house that became the school.

The address was Avenue Nader, *lote 13* (lot #13), because the municipality had not yet issued street numbers. Along with my hammock, I had my suitcase, some books and ESL materials, a folding table and chairs, a cooler, some pots, pans and tableware. The bedrooms had built-in mattress platforms made of cinderblock covered with cement; not having a mattress, I put all my belongings up on the platforms. This was a fortunate move, because a downpour came that first night, flooding the place. I lowered my feet out of the hammock into ankle-deep cold water.

By the afternoon the water had drained out, but I had to find out how it was getting in. The owner of my Parque las Palapas apartment was the only contractor I knew, so I asked him to investigate. He got up on the roof and walked around the perimeter of the house, ordering his two sons to lift one thing and tap on another. Shortly he came back with the pronouncement that under the foundation of the house lay a *cenote*, a spring-fed waterhole. He said I would have to buy and install a powerful pump to lower the water level of the *cenote* every time it rained.

Often I knew nothing about the subject at hand; still, I could usually sniff out nonsense, and this cenote-pump idea seemed expensive and ridiculous. I found a construction worker named Emilio down the block and brought him to see the house. He made the same rounds the contractor had, and shook his head. He couldn't figure out the cause of the flooding, he said, unless it was raining. I was willing to wait. The same evening, no sooner had the clouds burst but Emilio showed up. He found that a simple rain gutter and a chain were needed to conduct the torrents of rain away from the large, louvered window in the main room. This was a minor job to complete.

Soon I was ready to receive the school furniture I had ordered, the large chalkboard, the white conference table and the twenty blue plastic nesting chairs of the best quality. I lined the table up parallel with the red tiles on the floor, to make sure it was standing perfectly straight in the exact middle of the room. I hung a National Geographic world map on one wall, and a Grand Canyon poster on another. On a back door I stuck a curious poster of images from *La Lotería*—fifty-four colorful, art-deco style images of people, animals and objects. I plugged in my record player on top of a cabinet; below it, I stored my small collection of records and tapes: Beatles, Stones, Stevie Wonder, Joan Baez, Dylan and Tina Turner.

Near the record player I sat a little blonde doll on a painted toy chair. I arranged some bright paper mache fruit in a basket for "realia," objects students could handle and talk about. Then I stood with my hands on my hips and my back to the chalkboard, admiring my beautiful classroom.

 *12*   *Blondie to the Rescue*

Now what I needed at the school was students. My next step was to locate a printer to make promotional cards. I ordered one thousand cards with the Mayan glyph logo I had chosen, the name of the school, its meaning in Spanish and English, the location, and the date and hour of the first class. I had found the glyph on the cover of a book that had belonged to my mother, Sylvanus G. Morely's massive *The Ancient Maya*.

Escuela Xicalango, *El Lugar en Donde el Idioma Se Cambia*, "The Place Where the Language Charges," is how the flyers came out. I didn't notice the error, the "r" in place of "n" in the last word in English, until I had paid for the cards and taken them home. *¡Ay, dios!* I exclaimed, what kind of ad would this be? But before setting off to argue with the printer, it occurred to me that by extending one leg of the "r" with a black pen, I could make it into an "n." That night, one thousand "charges" became "changes," in "The Place Where the Language Changes."

ESCUELA XICALANGO

The Place Where the Language Changes
El lugar en donde el idioma se cambia

A Canadian neighbor told me that her husband supervised the lifeguard squad, and that they were in desperate need of English on the job. On a Wednesday morning I went to their headquarters and invited all sixteen young men to come for a free lesson that night. I was nervous and excited.

In the grocery store, at the bus stop and the handicraft market I handed out the flyers; no one asked me about the altered "r." That night at six, four tanned and muscular lifeguards appeared, wearing freshly ironed jeans and tee shirts, their hair still wet from showers. They took places on the blue chairs on both sides of the conference table and looked up at me.

Dr. Harvey Nadler, the chair of the ESL Teaching department at NYU, had impressed me with his ability to learn nearly one hundred names in one go-around; that's why I always made a point of learning all the students' names through a little name game on Day One, and seeing that the students did the same. With no more than twenty in a room, this game is just hard enough to make people laugh, which is a great way to get started. When everyone knows the names of their classmates, they feel free to talk to everyone else, again a great way to start.

After the names, my lesson plan for that evening continued with teaching the students the possessives my, your, his and her.

When a structure in your native language is very different from the related structure in the "target" language, the one you are learning, this is called a language conflict. The words "your," "his," and "her" are good examples, because the Spanish word, *"su"* can be used for all three: *Su nombre es Pedro* (His name is Pedro); *Su nombre es Elena* (Her name is Elena) and *Su nombre de usted es Ricardo, ¿verdad?* (Your name is Ricardo, right?)

So the lesson I had planned to teach on the first day was a difficult one because of the language conflict; but I hadn't thought about how difficult it would be without any female students in the group. Confidently I wrote on the board,

My ___ ___ ____.
Your ___ ___ ___.
His ___ ___ ____.

Her ___ ___ ___.

I said, "My name is Deborah," my thumb to my chest. I looked directly at one student and told him, "Your name is Sergio." I pointed to another man and faced the others, saying, "His name is Juan." Then I realized what was missing. My only option was to point to myself from the side and say, "Her name is Deborah."

"Now you," I suggested.

No one spoke. Their faces turned blank, the way mine does when someone talks about carburetors. Ten minutes into Xicalango's first class, I had lost my students.

Dr. Nadler at NYU had said, "Always make your students feel right. Don't ask them to do something unless you think they can." These strong young men had walked into the school smiling; now all four tanned foreheads were creased with anxiety. I looked around the room, searching for the girl student we didn't have.

My eyes settled on Blondie, the little cloth doll with yellow yarn hair and a stitched-on smile. Diablo had won her for Sandra by throwing balls into baskets in an Isla Mujeres fair, and Sandra had not found room for her in her suitcase. I picked her up from alongside the record player and propped her up against a dictionary on the table, saying, "Her name is Blondie." Suddenly our classroom was complete: the oldest of the four students raised his hand.

"My name is Juan," he said. "Your name is Déborah." He indicated a classmate with his thumb and said, "His name is Sergio." Then with a deep breath, he took one of Blondie's little feet between two fingers, and told us, "Her name is Blondie." I was careful to hide my sigh of relief.

The two students on the other side of the table spoke similar phrases. I set them to practicing as a pair, because next to the student named Juan, a diminutive young man with huge shoulders was motioning me to his side. "My tongue can't speak English," he whispered to me.

"Can you say "Cancún?" I asked him in Spanish.

"*Claro*, Cancún," he answered.

"Well, 'can' is an English word." I said. "It means *puedo*. Can you say 'okay?'"

"Okay."

"Can you say, 'Bye!'?"

"Bye."

"Great. Your tongue speaks English very well."

With a smile he turned to his partner and began practicing.

On Thursday night there were sixteen students, including three or four women. Twenty-three crowded into the room on Friday. We began the Social Friday tradition, listening to the Beatles at the end of class, and singing "Baby, You Can Drive My Car."

A few months later, one of the initial four students, the small fellow with the big shoulders, showed up between classes with an attractive wife and a gorgeous dark-haired baby girl in his arms.

"Congratulations!" I said. "What's her name?"

While the father gazed lovingly at the baby, his wife looked up at me and answered, "Blondie."

13 *Las Lunadas*

A folded note on lined paper torn from a child's notebook was sticking out from under my door. *"LUNADA HOY,"* it read in big letters. "Moonlight Beach Party Tonight. Punta Sam. Bring drinks or snacks, *botella o botana."*

I drove there with Diablo, who had introduced me to this *lunada* crowd. He was waiting on a bench in front of the school after the last classes let out, his head turning as each young woman stepped through the gate and onto the sidewalk of Avenue Nader.

In my VW bug, Diablo and I drove up Avenida Tulúm to the intersection called El Crucero, which marks the boundary between the town and *la colonia*. In this *barrio*, the houses had been built by their owners, often before streets were paved or utilities installed. A discount department store on the corner displayed an anagram of the intersection's name: El + 0 (+, *cruz*, the symbol of the cross, 0, zero, or *cero*). There we turned right on the Puerto Juarez Highway and passed a sliver of a market and a clutch of cinderblock houses. In no time Cancún lay behind us. Some tall palm trees and feathery pines lined the road. Corona *dispensarios* appeared every fifty yards or so.

We bumped over chunky *topes* (speed bumps), and approached the Puerto Juarez ferry landing and parking lots. Here we stopped to buy a bottle of Felipe II Brandy and a six-pack through a tiny barred window, like a quick visit to the penitentiary. Maybe it was a twelve-pack we bought; in any case, I'm sure they were *bien heladas* (really cold), the only way anyone would drink them.

The friends we were meeting worked at the airport as firemen and security guards, airline personnel and tower operators. Some were my students—FONATUR ran the airport. Most had arrived from Mexico City for the airport's opening in '74. By now they had houses, cars, spouses and babies, and they knew the ropes in Cancún. For example, they knew where you could get away with building a huge bonfire on the beach.

The car-ferry landing was in Punta Sam, five unlit kilometers north of Puerto Juarez. The ferry departed from Punta Sam for Isla Mujeres at ten in the morning and two in the afternoon, and returned at nine and one. Nothing else happened in Punta Sam in the whole day—at night, less than nothing. It was very easy to locate our *lunada*.

From the road we saw the glow of a bonfire and then the parked cars. I turned off the motor of my car and listened to the strong voices singing as sparks flew skyward. Diablo deposited the beers in a cooler and poured himself a drink before joining the crowd around the fire. I walked toward the water first.

The moon was low on the horizon; its reflection paved a shimmering path all the way to Isla Mujeres, five kilometers away. Little houses with flickering lights were bunched toward the north end of the island, and farther south were a couple of hotels and a lighthouse.

A fresh breeze was blowing; clouds sailed across the sky. The Milky Way arched overhead, a thick hammock of stars. We were three miles from the nearest house, eight miles from any sizable source of artificial light. The hotels of Cancún were illuminated by spotlights, but from here they were only shiny rhinestones on the horizon.

I saw the familiar constellations, and the Mayan constellations too, like the Scorpion, and the Tail of the Rattlesnake, as locals called the Pleiades. As the wind propelled the clouds toward the moon, they became velvety, dense as black holes. When the moon was hidden, distant stars shone with great brilliance. Some flashed crimson, yellow, purple. As the moon emerged again, the rim of the cloud glowed silver and lavender. Palm trees tossed their shining manes, graceful silhouettes against the star-strewn sky.

I poured myself a shot of tequila from a half-empty bottle and tossed it down, reveling in Don Sixto's voice and guitar. First he played *Mi Ciudad*, My City. Nearly everyone sang along, verse after verse. Heriberto joined him with a second guitar perfectly tuned to the first. Next came *No Volvere*, a tearjerker that the entire party belted out, with a full complement of Mexican *ay-ay-ays* and ironic sobbing:

Fuimos nubes el viento apartó, (we were clouds parted by the winds)

Fuimos piedras que siempre chocamos, (we were stones always crashing together)

Gotas de agua el sol resecó, (drops of water dried by sun)

Borracheras que no terminamos. (drunken parties that we never ended)

Don Sixto was a small, wiry fellow from *El Disastro Federal*, as he called Mexico D.F., about ten years older than the rest of us. He was a career fireman, and narrated stories of disasters with relish. His hatchet nose and pitch-black hair might have come from Tarascan ancestors, from Michoacán, and his musical skill too.

So we sang! We drank! We smoked! We pulled blankets around each other, huddled and cuddled. After a time, people started to ask where the food was. Some got up and started rooting about for it, but what for? It became apparent that everyone had brought *botella*, and no one had brought *botana*. What a laugh we got out of that! More driftwood was piled on the fire. Now we sang *La Bamba* and danced to keep warm.

The dawn awakened me. I had fallen asleep with my hard contact lenses in place, and my eyelids were nearly stuck together. Slowly I extricated myself from the blanket two others were still sleeping under. People were strewn about like silent driftwood, except for those who were snoring.

¡Qué buena lunada! We didn't have parties like this in Brooklyn.

14 Skeletons of the Maya

The islands now called Isla Mujeres and Cozumel were sacred to the ancient Mayans, with their temples dedicated to Ixchel, goddess of the moon and fertility. Women wishing to bear children made pilgrimages there. I knew a small temple on the grounds of Hotel Camino Real, and I had heard that others had been covered over during the hotel's construction. On the road to Punta Sam the ruins known as El Meco were under excavation. Cancún held more ruins, I had been told, and I wanted to see them all.

One weekend early in my first year in Cancún, I treated myself to a motorboat tour of the Laguna Nichupte, a tour that culminated in a visit to the post-classic Mayan site known as *las Ruinas del Rey*. Minutes after setting off from the roadside pier, the little launch began threading through winding channels, among protruding mangrove roots. Snowy egrets floated upward from branch to higher branch as we approached; a green heron ducked back into the foliage and disappeared in eerie shadows. Now the tourists stopped chattering. Something gray, rutted as a dead tree and nearly as long as a canoe, submerged itself at the sound of the motor.

Abruptly, sky and water opened wide before us. The broad lagoon reflected a brilliant noon sky, and the lanchero revved the engine. We zoomed toward our destination, the solitary pier alongside *las ruinas*. No other boat was tied up there. Indeed, there were no other boats on the entire shining expanse of lagoon.

On foot now, the guide took up the head of our single file away from the lagoon, under the angular almond trees. Around us all was green—emerald green, jade green, bottle green, as if we had stepped into a giant bowl of salad. The siricote blossoms stood out like cherry tomatoes, and the *flamboyán* tree branches formed a leafy arch over our heads. After a while the path entered a clearing, and we stood facing an assemblage of dappled gray structures of different sizes set in mossy green, like gemstones on velvet. There were flat-topped pyramids and minuscule square stone houses with tiny doorways, exactly the right size for the *yucateco* version of the "little people," the *aluxes*. These "small ones" guard the cornfields, students told me, and would urinate on poachers, and poke sharp fingers into the sides of anyone who tried to sleep where he didn't belong. They were also guardians of the ancient cities.

I saw platforms with colonnades, miniature versions of structures I knew from Chichén Itzá and Tulúm. All the lichen-spotted buildings looked as if they had grown there, appendages on an ancient skeleton beneath the grass.

Shading one platform was a leaf-green palapa roof woven of palm fronds. Its color betrayed how new it was, as after a week or two palapas turn brown. The guide advised us not to walk up that set of stone steps—he said archeologists were at work there, reassembling the steps around it and digging up the floor. But today was a Sunday; no one was working, and the calm around me spread through me. I roamed alone from one end to the other, photographing painted surfaces, *bas reliefs*, butterflies. Shortly the guide rounded us up, long before I was ready to go.

One week later, after driving back and forth to my classes in the hotel zone all week, I felt ready for a long hike to the *ruinas*. I decided against taking my camera on such a sandy trek. A dirt road was open as far as the President's Casa Maya, and then I would walk a much more rustic path. I parked under palms and started off on foot, stepping over fallen coconut trunks and around young plants.

Coconuts grow so easily. Wherever a coconut falls on the sand, it can take root. The sprout nourishes itself on the coconut meat until the roots find enough water beneath the sand. Sturdy chartreuse fronds were sprouting from coco heads at every step. The path was a sandy obstacle course.

After a while the mosquitoes were too much for me, so I made my way across a narrow area of jungle and then over the dunes. From the ridge I could see there was no one on the path, and no one on the beach. A plane passed, on its way to New York, I thought. I waved. If anyone sees me, I smiled to myself, they'll think I'm a castaway.

At last I reached the ruins; there was no one in sight. It seemed the guards had Sundays off. I climbed the small pyramids and ducked into the little houses. An artisan who carved Mayan glyphs and *bas reliefs* in limestone had shown me a plant with skinny, red fingerlike flowers that would tint a white stone pink. I plucked leaves, rolled them between my palms and rubbed them on a stone I found. It turned rosy, sure enough.

Bushes were hung with great bunches of sea grapes. With the hint of the salt water they had sucked from the sandy soil, the small purplish-red globes held a juice tangy as wine. Sea grape leaves are rubbery disks. Resting a leaf on a stone step, I scratched my name on one with a twig, in the calligraphic script my Uncle Arturo had taught me. Resin in the leaf turned the letters white. Then I added my drawing of how most people pronounced my last name. Like an anagram, the leaf read: Deborah Fish.

Just behind the sea grape was the structure where archeologists had been working. This time there was no one to warn me not to step on the loose stones. The drying palapa roof would provide some shade. What were the archeologists digging for, I wondered.

Several holes about a foot in diameter pierced the smooth floor. Inside the first hole I saw a skull. No, not just a skull, it was a complete skeleton, bony knees pulled up to bony chin. The skeleton seemed to be intact, inside a large ceramic urn. I could see the terracotta inner wall of the urn; dirt was packed around the outside. Turning, I peered into the next hole—another skeleton! This one was smaller, and it appeared intact, too. It must have been a small adult, probably a woman. I imagined her walking in among those ruins, taking small steps in her sandals and huipil. I felt a kinship with her. How had she died, and why was she buried in the floor of a temple?

Now I turned to the other holes—there were five in all, and each one had an urn with a skeleton inside. Was there gold inside the urns, was there jade? Why hadn't I brought my camera, I reprimanded myself. I could only document these burials within my memory.

I wondered who else knew about this find. I'll come back next week with my camera, I promised myself.

I think two weeks went by before I returned. The palapa roof of the little temple was now cream-colored and dry. And the temple had a smooth new cement floor. There were no holes, no urns, no skeletons, not a trace of what I had seen. And still no guards or other tour groups or guides to talk to.

Quite some time later a Museum of Anthropology and Archeology opened next to the Convention Center in the hotel zone. Finally I could ask someone what had happened to the skeletons that were excavated at the Ruinas del Rey.

"Skeletons?" the young lady asked me back. "There were no skeletons discovered at las Ruinas del Rey. *Nada. No, nada.*" And that was all.

 *Book 1 , Unit 5*

Some students leaned forward, others craned their necks trying to see what I was drawing on the board. It was a cartoon of me in a sailboat, arm in arm with a handsome man. There was a drink in my hand and a bowl on a table in front of us.

In our long, narrow classroom, with its windows facing Avenue Nader on one end and the chalkboard on the other, eighteen students sat around the white conference table. This setup worked well in most respects; everyone could see and listen to their teacher and classmates, and they could work in pairs with the classmate to one side. But for the students halfway down the table to see the board was a challenge; Rigo stretched his head up to see over Anamaria's bouffant, then ducked again.

It was only the fifth week of the term, but already we knew a great deal about each other, in English. We all knew each other's first and last names and that Déborah is from Brooklyn, Amalia is

from Acapulco and Juanito is from Tixcoco'ob. We knew where each one worked, who was married, who had children and who was single.

Our books, *New Horizons in English*, taught us the colors and the articles of clothing, giving student models the chance to sashay down imaginary runways while a student MC crooned: "Elvia is wearing a blue tank top, a pink skirt and yellow platform flipflops," or "Abrám's soccer jersey is red, white and green."

Who, What, Where and When were new tools we learned to use in Unit 3, along with telling time and locating objects. Now we knew what was in Luli's kitchen and who was sitting on her sofa.

Unit 4 represented a giant step: using what we learned in this chapter, we could describe our classmates in all their sun-tanned good looks. I was charmed to hear for the first time in my life that I was "tall." The book's alternatives for describing physiques were "chubby, thin or just right." I translated "just right" for them as "*como mango.*" I soon learned that most of the women in the school, myself included, fit into the category called "just right." Using the structures and vocabulary students learned in this unit, they could play "I'm a famous person," and guess that Orlando was standing in for Donna Summer, and that Rufino was President Jimmy Carter.

But Unit 5 was liberation. We could talk about what we liked and what we didn't like, starting with food and drink, then going on to restaurants, stores, parks, beaches, music and more. We practiced buying food and drink, listing the ingredients we purchased until someone could guess that Nelly was making enchiladas suizas and Ramón was preparing piña coladas.

Then we played a charades game called "I'm hungry!" I'd direct a student to ask the class what I was doing, while I pretended to crack peanuts between my fingers, or to drink a Tecate beer from an invisible can, with lime juice and salt sprinkled on the top. They would top me then, pantomiming chomping on crunchy tacos of *chicharrón* (fried pork rinds). One pretended to drink coconut juice straight from the coco, after shinnying up the palm tree, hacking at the coconut's stem, dropping it to the ground and shearing off the top with an imaginary machete.

In an earlier chapter they had learned "wearing," "sitting" and "reading." They had "sat" on the backs of horses, they had "read" comic books, cookbooks and tearjerkers. At the end of Unit 5, they knew enough so that they could write a prose poem, a perfect moment encapsulated.

"Debby's Dream," I called mine, and I wrote and illustrated it in blue and white chalk on the board. I wrote:

It is three o'clock in the afternoon.

I'm sitting on my sailboat.

I'm wearing a blue bikini and Coppertone #4.

I'm eating ceviche.

I'm drinking a Cuba Libre.

I'm sitting next to my boyfriend.

A petite Campeche teenager, one who had tiptoed to her seat the first days of class, wrote:

I'm sitting on my motorcycle.

I'm wearing a leather skirt.

I'm riding back to my hometown.

Other students gazed pensively at the ceiling, then wrote:

I'm eating lobster tacos. I'm sitting at the best table in my own restaurant.

Spanish/English dictionaries circulated around our conference table and hands flew up in the air, as each sought the exact words that would make his or her dream authentic. They wrote:

I'm wearing blue jeans and cowboy boots.

I'm sitting on my white stallion.

I'm sitting on the terrace of a penthouse.

I'm looking at the golf course.

I'm sitting next to the groom at my wedding.
I'm listening to a mariachi band.

I'm sitting on the side of my swimming pool.
I'm reading a book. I wrote the book.

I'm sitting on my bicycle.
I'm wearing a yellow jersey.
I'm riding in the Tour de France.

I'm sitting in the cabin of my airplane.
I'm listening to a piano.

In our fifth week of class, with our little bit of English, we dreamed great dreams...

16 Starry Night

Friends came by frequently after classes were over for the day. One evening, five of us were listening to records in the biggest classroom. Three were divers from Cozumel: Goldie and his friends Beto-van and El Guiri-Guiri. Elaine, a new teacher with a great sense of humor, was there, too. We played Stevie Wonder, Janis Joplin, the Stones. We pushed the table and chairs against the walls, as we did for dance-parties. I was leaning back, arm extended in a fast swing with my partner, when the music stopped abruptly and the lights went out.

This was nothing unusual for us. I doubt that a week went by without some kind of power outage. And why would we mind, anyway? When there was no artificial light, the lightshow in the sky was mind-bending.

This particular night was cool and clear. It was easy to discern the green, yellow or scarlet of twinkling stars on nights like this one. I had learned a few constellations from H.A. Rey's *The Stars, a New Way to See Them*. I knew *Ursa Mayor*, the Big Dipper, and Orion's belt, *El Cinto de Orion*. Beto-van had just pointed the Perseids out, so we were all looking in that direction, when the customarily facetious Elaine pointed a finger and said quietly, "That star is coming closer."

Someone speculated, "Maybe it's a plane."

"It can't be a plane."

"I think it's a satellite."

"Definitely not."

"Well, there's no question that it's coming closer. I think it's moving too fast to be a plane."

"Do you think it could it be…" someone was musing, when my heart thumped and my jaw dropped—the star veered off its course at a ninety degree angle. It zoomed across the sky. When it was completely gone from sight, the streetlights burst back on. Every light in the school was burning.

We argued as we entered the building. Back inside, we continued our dispute into the night.

"A helicopter can't move like that."

"Well, how about a satellite?"

"Impossible."

"Well, then, maybe a…"

The only thing we didn't disagree about was whether we had seen it. All five of us were certain we had seen it.

 *Counting Money*

I sat at the head of the white conference table, counting money. It was just after nine in the evening and a full day of student registration was behind me.

Xicalango now had three classrooms, and there were six class periods each day. Some teachers taught all six periods. I usually taught the first two and the last two; others taught mornings or evenings only.

Early students would arrive freshly showered and neatly groomed at seven-thirty in the morning. Like little else in Cancún, classes at Escuela Xicalango began and ended punctually, so that students could arrive at work on time. They left the classrooms at eight-fifty, and a second group entered, this shift bubbling with bouncy young mothers chatting about the kids they had just dropped off at school.

"*¡Mañana tú me haces la votada!*" one beauty called out to another as they took seats on opposite sides of the table, literally, "You throw my kids out along with yours tomorrow, okay?"

The third morning shift, ten-thirty to noon, was smaller and worldlier—here we saw the bartenders, the slender Hawaiian dancers from the show at Mauna Loa, the midnight taxi drivers. The dancers primped for the dj's; waiters vied to sit alongside manicured restaurant hostesses.

Early afternoon classes, four-thirty to five-fifty, tended to run to extremes. High school boys and girls sat next to morning-shift policemen and security guards, goofy good-nature vs. serious purpose.

During rainy seasons I pitied the students who arrived for the six p.m. classes, at *la hora del mosquito.* We couldn't let students enter the classrooms early; every room was already packed with the previous shift. Sometimes I'd be in front of the school at that hour, speaking with a teacher or a student. Suddenly irritated, I would glance at my ankles to find dozens of mosquitoes attacking me. Students beat at their legs with notebooks; they swore they'd never wear short-shorts again.

The classes from six p.m. to seven-twenty were the most crowded, with students of all ages and from every sector of Cancún's population. From seven-thirty to nine in the evening, most students were single twenty-somethings, and flaunting it.

The way they dressed for school amused me. Sometimes a prim and proper young lady would show up in a black lace blouse with a red bra underneath. One wore a tee shirt I knew she didn't understand. It showed a woozy kitten propped up inside a full cocktail glass. The words on it read, "Happiness is a Tight Pussy."

These were the years of miniskirts and hot pants, and nowhere were they better worn, or better received, than in Cancún. The young men loved to pull their tee shirts up above their nipples, exposing coppery six-packs. It must have been the heat.

On registration days, a secretary and several teachers would be on hand. We would give new entrants an oral test to determine their level of English proficiency. But for returning students all we had to give them was an enthusiastic welcome.

Registration lasted all day, and often by evening we were turning students away—no more room in that level, at that hour, we had to tell them. "Any chance you could change your shift at work?" we'd ask.

The secretary would put cash into a hinged wooden box I had brought with me from New York, an antique that had been made for Celia Frisch, the grandmother I'd never met. It bore her initials among the carved art deco designs on the lid, and was lined in red felt. The peso bills inside were of many colors, different sizes, and many smells too. Everything in Cancún smelled at least a little of sweat.

That evening, the counting almost finished, thousands of pesos were sitting in colorful stacks before me when the door opened again. Two tall young men, each no more handsome than a Greek god, stepped inside. One I recognized from the windsurfing crowd—blond, deeply tanned, he was a successful restaurant owner. In the white tee shirt printed with the Mayan logo of his restaurant, he glowed in the doorway. The other was dark-haired, of a type I associated with Zapotec royalty: finely carved nose, straight hair falling to broad shoulders, eyes the color of espresso. All the confidence there has ever been on this earth rose into the air from his brilliant white smile.

"We want to register for classes," Zapotec Prince had come to tell me. "When do they begin? How long will it take my slow-witted friend over here to learn a little?"

The other asked, "Will you be our teacher? We want *you* to be our teacher."

I answered their questions and registered them, trying hard not to shake my head in astonishment. *"¿Quién como tú, Déborah?"* I asked myself over and over. Who's got it like you do?

18 *A Six-pointed Starfish*

At the banquet after my childhood friend Arlene's wedding in 1980 and on subsequent visits to her home in Orlando, Florida, she kept trying to convince me to move there. The business her husband Nathan had started was really taking off, she said. She pointed out that a large segment of Orlando's population needed to learn English, and that her new town, like Cancún, was booming.

Although Arlene and Nathan had met at a nonsectarian mixer, once married they began studying Judaism; they were more conservative in every respect each time I saw them. Consequently, Arlene seemed anxious to introduce me to a Jewish guy. She was concerned I would never meet one in Cancún.

One day while snorkeling during my midday break, I spotted a lovely yellow starfish on the ocean floor, a six-pointed starfish. I dove down for it, took it home and dried it in the sun. Once it was stiff as plaster and odor-free, I mailed it to Arlene, with a card saying, "I hope you like this Jewish Star-Fish. You see, I'm not the only one in the Caribbean."

But treatment of the Jewish Guy topic became more serious on the next visit. At dinner Nathan brought up the names of more friends. I can't say I was interested, but still I became angry when Arlene countered one suggestion with, "No, Nathan, not Lewis!"

"Why not Lewis?" he asked.

"Nathan, because of their religious differences!"

"Wait a second," I interrupted, "we're both Jewish, right?"

She gave me a hard look.

After their daughter was born, I made a short visit, wanting to enjoy their new baby with them. The second afternoon, while

Nathan was at work and Arlene and the baby were upstairs, the doorbell rang. I answered it, and spoke to the man at the door; I think he was a deliveryman with a present for the baby. While the door was open, Arlene appeared on the stairs and asked me to come and talk to her as soon as I was available.

I did, and found her furious.

"In this house we do not open the door for people we don't know," she said.

I was caught off-guard. "Why not?" I asked.

"Because they might want to rob us!" she exclaimed.

I could not digest this information. At my home, which was also my school, I invited all of Cancún inside, every day from Monday to Friday, and I felt comfortable doing so. If my friend in her luxurious suburban home couldn't open the door to people, then there was no question in my mind as to who was living well and who wasn't.

19 *Flight to Miami*

The Mexican Immigration Service required that gringos like me leave the country every six months to apply for new visas. In Cancún I always seemed to be in the midst of chattering clusters of people, classes or groups of friends. But for an expensive, obligatory trip to Miami I had no choice but to fly alone.

Check-in was interminable, and as usual, the air-conditioning was *en reparación*. I nudged my suitcase one inch forward, half an inch, another little bit. Ahead of me I heard familiar voices from a cheery little clique. At its center stood a Mexican couple I knew, both tennis pros at a luxury hotel. They looked like stars of some Mexican soap opera, *una novela*, with their thick, glossy hair and their perfect physiques. They were joking with three tanned young men in pastel LaCoste shirts and shorts that showed off muscular calves and thighs. I imagined where I would position myself in that circle: between the broad-shouldered *chilango*, a Mexico City lawyer I had met at the FONATUR office, and the witty redhead with the left-handed serve. But their huddle was self-absorbed; no one noticed me way back in the line.

I glanced again at the *Newsweek* magazine I had bought for the ninety-minute flight. There was an aerial photo of a dismembered jet plane on the cover. I rolled the magazine into a tube; I'd open it later, maybe...

Threading down the narrow aisle toward the rear of the plane, I greeted the gang of five. The *chilango* gave me a white-toothed grin and *Señor* and *Señora Novela* winked at me, the tennis teacher's salute. There were no empty seats near them, nothing until the next-to-last row. I took the window seat on the ocean side, and settled the *Newsweek* on the adjacent vacant seat. A smooth-haired airline hostess passed, reminding passengers to straighten their seat backs and prepare for take-off. The two seats behind me were empty. Then the other hostess left her folded blue jacket on one.

We took off heading north. Once aloft I could see the new white one-, two- and three-story buildings of the town. Then I shuddered at the clump-clump of the landing wheels entering the body of the plane; I always forgot what that sound was, until it had unnerved me again.

Once I located Avenue Tulúm, it was easy to find my street, Avenida Nader, encircling my neighborhood, *la Manzana Tres*. I saw my brick schoolhouse and home—I even saw my mango tree in the back yard. My place was less than one block from the *Palacio Municipal* with its radio tower. The town looked so small.

Just to the east of town there was a border of marshy green *area verde*, and then the water. That morning the sea was transparent aquamarine where white sand lay below, and darker where turtle grass grew on the ocean floor. We gained altitude; I could see patterns of currents marked in indigo and cobalt. Where the water was shallow, I saw the golden color of elkhorn coral reef below. Then I realized that the reef I was looking at in front of Vacation Club International was the spot where I had snorkeled the day before. In my mind I saw a parrotfish I had noticed, its face like a Peter Max design, chomping on a branch of coral; I could even hear it. It was thrilling to be so high above and so cool below at the same time.

Then the plane rose above the clouds. I opened my tray table and rolled my *Newsweek* the opposite way to flatten it.

An article about the recent spate of airline disasters, what Mexicans call *avionazos*, was staring at me: O'Hare—Black box missing. American Airlines—Firestorm. Tenerife—Wind shear. Japan— Terrorists. No survivors. A litany of locations and casualties, causes and mysteries, the bereaved and the enraged. My eyes ached.

A sweet airline attendant with a hot *torta*, a sandwich in a crusty roll, interrupted my anxiety. Her ebony eyes shone as she invited me to try a complimentary *"tequilazo."* Such confidence these young women exude, in themselves, the pilot, the airplane, even in a passenger, me. The second hostess passed the first with a little *"Permisito."* She reminded me of Carmen Miranda, with her sexy smile under dark curls round as grapes.

I downed my tequila in one shot and felt a burst of anticipation for my trip; I devoured my chipotle leg-of-pork torta, managing miraculously to avoid getting crumbs down my neckline. I uncurled the magazine again, this time to a review of a new movie, *Annie Hall.* I can see it in Miami, I thought. Cancún's single movie theater never showed Woody Allen.

"In just a few minutes we will beguine our descent into Miami." When they begin the beguine, I smiled to myself.

Then the magazine jumped up in my face. The whole plane had jumped. Lurched. My heart too.

One stewardess and then the other ran to refuge in the seats behind me. "Have you *e*-ver felt anything like that?" Torta Queen asked Carmen.

"NO, *NE*-ver!" Another wrenching bounce. Overhead compartment doors snapped open. Some passengers yelled, and someone was retching. Across the aisle I heard, *"Padre Nuestro que está en el cielo bendito sea su nombre..."* (our Father who art in heaven…)

More lateral shaking. A crunch. A hop. Two more sideways lurches. In panic I sneaked a look out the tilted window at blue Biscayne Bay. There were no signs of apocalypse below. My breath was loud in my ears.

The lurching eased off and finally we landed, with some hard bounces on the runway. Passengers gasped, then groaned in relief. Some began to applaud. Attendant Carmen shepherded an old woman toward the door with an arm around her waist. My Torta Queen had recovered her composure and wished me a pleasant stay in Miami or my final destination. Was I the only one whose hands still trembled?

At the baggage carousel the five friends stood laughing and joking, just as they had in Cancún. "What did you think about that bouncing just before we landed?" I asked them, wide-eyed.

"Wha-a-a-t?" *Señor Novela* grinned at me, teeth as even as Chiclets. "You mean the speed bumps?"

I snorted with laughter, and then we all laughed, and looked at each other laughing, the six of us, and laughed some more. The redhead picked my bag up off the carousel with his left hand, and his friends began making jibes about *zurdos* (lefties) and *sordos* (the deaf), and *izquierdistas* (leftists) while we waited for the other bags. Then we all walked toward the exit together. Next to the sliding door in front of the taxi stands, I threw that *pinche Newsweek* magazine in the trash!

This speed-bump joke was a typical Mexican response to near-disaster, and to disaster as well. Mexico is the earthquake-shaken country where, before the dust settles, the jokes begin to rise. When you ask a Mexican couple how they're doing, he hugs her and they chuckle, *"Jodidos pero contentos."* Fucked, but happy. *¡Viva Mexico!*

 # 20 Can Mexican Magic Work on American Men?

Not long after the school was established I got a letter from a tall, attractive friend I'd met at a school where I'd worked in New York. He wrote that he would like to visit me in Cancún and then go on to Cozumel for some diving. He had been a popular history teacher and administrator at the school; he was also a published author and a black belt in karate. We had gone out for lunch together several times and to a play once, but I don't think either of us had any serious intentions about the other.

When I spotted Mark at the airport, his wiry black hair was oddly awry, and his black beard accentuated his New York pallor. I didn't hear any joy in his voice at being on vacation in this brand-new resort, or at seeing me again. On the drive to Cancún from the airport he told me that his new novel had been accepted for publication some time back, but that the editor was just sitting on it. This was the reason he was so preoccupied, he told me.

Later that day, as we jogged between flowering oleander bushes on the winding bicycle path, Mark spoke more about his frustration. In the evening while dining on ceviche and scrumptious jumbo shrimp in garlic sauce, he told me how impossible it was to begin a new writing project until publication of the last one was assured. Even when we were dancing at Krakatoa, the most atmospheric disco in Cancún, this talented and musical young man couldn't get into the music with me; we danced together as if we were on stilts.

Then someone else had enough nerve to come to our table and ask me to dance. It was Rafael, an *acapulqueño* who sold silver jewelry on the beach. Well, I think he sold silver jewelry, but I'm sure he sold alpaca. Alpaca is nickel silver, a metal alloy known in Mexico as *chafa*, or "cheap stuff." Many beach salesmen sell *chafa por plata*, that is, they tell the customers they're buying silver at a great price, but what they're getting is alpaca. The first time I met Rafael, he sold me a twisty little silver bracelet and made a big production of telling me that it was the real thing, and that I was getting it at the home-girl price.

Rafael was from the area they call *"la costa chica,"* on the Pacific coast near Acapulco, where the people are of mixed race, descendants of African slaves and indigenous people. We had danced together at Krakatoa before, and I was thrilled to be on the dance floor with him again. He was a creative dancer, whirling me in complex combinations I had not tried before. Although he was short and slight, he was a masterful partner; with Rafa leading, I never took a misstep.

There was something else too; when the music turned from salsa to rock and we began dancing separately, I realized that all his moves began in his hips and radiated outward to his shoulders, head, arms and legs. They radiated to me, too. He was wearing slim, dark jeans with white stitching, so the stitches on the flap over the zipper stood out. When the black lights flashed, so did that dancing zipper. I moved in perfect sync with him, and other couples on the floor seemed get a thrill from watching us. It felt as if we were at a party with a dancefloor full of uninhibited friends.

But Mark was not one. Returning to the table, I was worried he would be annoyed with me for dancing so sexily with an interloper. But it turned out he hadn't even noticed; instead, he told me what he was going to do to that editor. She had a long ponytail, he told me, and he was going to cut it off!

I had nothing to say to Mark. As I sat sipping my mai tai and watching Rafael lead another girl, this is what I realized: Rafael's greatest asset was his self-confidence. It was visible in the way he danced and in his knack for talking to people. He didn't focus on what was lacking, but did his best with what he had. I was a New Yorker, so I had spent most of my life thinking and talking about deficits and problems. Political issues, family problems, housing difficulties, man trouble, lack-of-man trouble, money issues, job disputes, psychological problems that lead to other problems or vice versa. That's what my New York friends and I talked about endlessly, what we went to psychologists and therapy groups to talk about, even what we dreamed about.

Meanwhile, problems are the last thing Mexicans want to talk about. I think problems are taboo in polite conversation. You can make jokes about them, but that's all. Of course people think about their problems—but does anyone ever talk about them? *¡Jamás!* Never!

My students liked talking about the opposite sex, but with fantasy and humor. They loved talking about their tastes and preferences in food, clothing, cars, places to go. They talked about parties, the ones they had been to recently, and the ones coming up soon. Men loved to talk about sharks, tarantulas, fer-de-lance snakes and other killers they claimed to encounter every day of the week. They talked about wild fun at work and at home. But to talk about a problem would be like coming to class with a big, greasy stain on your shirt, something that had dripped out of your taco.

Mark's vacation plan, as he had mentioned in his letter, was to spend two days with me, then a week in Cozumel, diving. I was happy to see him go.

And even happier to greet him on his return—Mark came back a new man. The beard was trimmed, the hair was tied in a ponytail, and his skin had turned dark brown! I guess it might have crossed my mind in New York that his hair and facial features had an African-American look to them, but I didn't think about it. At my door in Cancún this time, he had a big grin on his face and a complexion like Sidney Poitier's. Six days on a dive boat had brought out his color and spirit.

The diving had been fantastic, he said. The visibility was excellent at Palancar reef, where the water was six hundred feet deep. There were sharks everywhere you looked. His companions on the diving trips were a bunch of jokers from Texas and California, and they had partied together night after night.

A footnote: I got a funny thank-you letter from Mark a few weeks later. After he returned to New York he had gone to visit his mother at her apartment. She opened the door, and then nearly slammed it in his face—at first she didn't recognize the tall African-American man standing there. But Mark laughed this off, and seemed relaxed about the publishing situation and everything else—Mexico had worked its magic.

21 Thanksgiving with Daniel

Daniel came to Thanksgiving at Escuela Xicalango on the invitation of my French friend Yvette. She had met him on the ferry to Isla Mujeres and thought he seemed *"absolument gentil."* Once I met him, I agreed. He spoke animatedly in awful Spanish or hip English with everyone at the feast. Between bouts of volubility he seemed oddly overwhelmed with the gathering. He explained that he had just left a Mayan town where he had been filming a documentary for the previous six months. This dinner was his first foray into the twentieth century in half a year, and he was delighting in it.

Once the dinner was finished and people started to gather the platters on which they had brought their potluck offerings, Daniel took me aside. "Now I can make my contribution," he told me seriously. "I'll wash all the dishes," he said, "if you'll stand next to me and talk."

What a generous offer—of course I would.

"Tell me how you got down here," Daniel asked, "and how you happened to open this school." That took quite some time, with him drawing me out and commenting all along. Then I got to ask the questions, starting with what else he had filmed. Well, an expedition to the top of Mount Everest, an artists' community on an island off the coast of France; he had filmed in jungles and on desert caravans.

"Not the moon?" I wondered aloud.

"Not yet," he replied.

Like me, Daniel was Jewish. He grew up in Michigan, where he had one brother. His mother had died of cancer, mine of leukemia.

We had both been adrift on a motherless sea, but we had each found work we loved, to which we could anchor ourselves.

His slim figure twisted gracefully from the sink; he was able to give me full attention, and polish off monumental stacks of dishes, great vats of greasy forks and spoons at the same time. We were making headway.

Daniel had loved living with the Mayans. He spoke a bit of Mayan. He knew, as I did, that they are very hard workers, and very funny. They have outrageous ways of flirting with girls, he told me. If some girls are going to swim in a *cenote*, a water hole, the boys will ask them innocently, "Oh, are you on your way to wash that cute little thing of yours?"

He had messy black hair and large eyes the color of beach glass, the glass that comes from Heineken bottles. We agreed that, in the Yucatán, those *ojos de colores* (eyes of colors other than brown or black) could do wonders for a person's popularity.

Dishes stacked and drying, we agreed to meet on Friday at noon for a run on the beach. Perhaps there were twenty hotels at that time, in 1977 or 1978. On that gray day we drove to Garza Blanca, the last hotel on the Caribbean side. A northerly was blowing, which meant rough water on the other beach, along the Bahia de Mujeres. On this side, only subdued swells reached our feet where we ran, just at the edge of the water, on the only hard sand along the beach.

Hard but smooth. The sand in Cancún is pulverized coral, very white. It's been smashed to tiny grains and polished by endless tossing in countless waves. They call it "air-conditioned sand," because it never burns the soles of your feet. Where it's dry, you sink into it up to your ankles with each step; at the water's edge it's a firm, tilted track.

I usually ran every school day around noon, between the morning and evening sessions. Eventually I realized that the experience—the sea, the beach, the wind, the clouds, the birds, my ideas—it was always new. Usually I ran alone. Sometimes a friend joined me, the kind of friend who could talk while running. Always I swam before beginning. My body cool, I would start running with

a song in my head. I never used a Walkman or any other music
player; music I loved would start to play with my first step. The
music might play in the foreground, while I sang the words silently,
or it might play in the background and allow me to think. These
were my most creative hours. When I reached Casa Maya, I always
plunged in once more to swim or play in the waves before turning
back.

Daniel and I talked as we ran, and stayed apace, but we weren't
well enough coordinated for his taste. His stride was much longer
than mine. To make up for it, he linked his arm with mine. Now
we ran right legs forward, then lefts. His left arm passed under my
right, touching my ribs. We ran like two horses yoked together,
faster than I ever had. Smoother. More buoyant. All the way to the
Casa Maya.

There we plunged our sweaty bodies into the turquoise waves.
Out where the water reached my breasts, he kissed me. He held
me. The waves hit us hard, and we laughed.

Back at home, we showered together in my little shower stall,
and he soaped the groove down the middle of my back. We made
love in my hammock and fell out of it. The next day we made love
on a sunfish sailboat and turned it over. We made love on the roof,
taking turns beaming back at the stars.

Daniel and I dressed in linen and silk for dinner in seafood
joints. We sucked sweet juice from each crab leg, and downed huge
goblets of a fish cocktail called *"Vuelve a la Vida."* (Come back to
life.) We drank wine. We were wine.

Several days passed. Just a few days and nights. He didn't really
have to live in California, Daniel told me —producers could get in
touch with him just as well in Cancún, so this could be his base. I
had talked about adding more rooms—more classrooms and more
living space. He asked if I wanted him to give me money for that
project. Proud of my earning capacity, I told him there was no
need.

Daniel told me there was a girl in California, in Pacific
Palisades. He had bought a house with her. But he would soon be

back with me. Around Christmas. Or just after Christmas. He had to return there now, he had been away for six months. He'd be back very soon. He gave me the phone number in Pacific Palisades.

I drove Daniel to the airport, quite a small airport then. I stood next to him right up to the gate, our arms encircling each other. We kissed fiercely at the gate, with the airline attendants and passengers all around us. Then the doors opened and he moved toward the plane, mostly walking backwards, waving. My heart leapt out of my chest toward him, and I followed it, running along the macadam toward the small group about to mount the stairs into the plane. I could hear the attendants calling me. But I ran.

"You run like a little deer," Daniel said with a smile as I came near him. Out on the runway we held each other one last time.

Airline officials approached.

I returned to the gate.

Daniel had said he would come around Christmas, or maybe in January. Then my father and my friend Anne and her boyfriend wrote that they wanted to come in January. I was waiting for Daniel's letter. They were coming and he was coming and I didn't know if I was coming or going. So I decided to call. But I didn't want to call. He had told me about a girlfriend, and I didn't want to talk to her.

I asked my friend Odalys to call. We must have gone to a public phone office, because this was years before I got a phone of my own. Odalys doesn't speak English, but I told her, "All you have to do if a woman answers the phone is say, 'Hello, may I speak with Daniel, please'."

A woman did answer. Odalys said her lines and then the woman said something Odalys didn't understand. Odalys kept asking, "What? What?" and I squeezed one hand and then the other in desperation; I can feel the pain of that moment right now. I took the phone from Odalys and spoke the simple request I believed would protect me, "May I speak with Daniel, please." The woman was sobbing on the other end of the phone line. She said,

"Who are you? Why are you calling Daniel? Daniel loves me. Why are you calling him?" I quietly hung up the phone.

I never saw Daniel again.

I can't swear it is true, but I believe I never telephoned a man I was missing again. What I'm sure is true is this: I forced myself to stop pining after people who were not there.

22 Moses and I Discover the Island

Moses, my best friend from City College, the Romanian/Israeli guy who had entertained me and my mother with his ironic stories, drove from New York City to Cancún several times, just to hang out. He had become good friends with my first Mexican boyfriend, Paco, and with Diablo, too. I had driven that route once—to make such an epic journey several times *está cabrón*.

On one of his visits we headed down to Belize, where we ran into some hippie types lounging in Belize City's Market Square, awaiting buyers for their big, old American cars. They lolled about, drinking cokes and smoking cigarettes in front of crusty GM station wagons with the wood-patterned vinyl peeling off the sides or pinkish Chevy sedans that had once been red. Cars were very expensive in Belize, especially big ones, and the right small-business man might pay royally for a Lincoln Continental with a snakeskin fade pattern or a Ford Fairlane jalopy.

Jalopy! Did Moses know jalopies? He knew enough to go to the Official Auction of the City of New York, held in the Bronx, and bid on a three-ton fire chief's station wagon. It was a 1966 Chevy Impala, red as an overripe tomato, complete with siren and bubblegum machine on the top. He bid two hundred dollars, and so did a gentleman built like the Chevy, but vertical. Moses is six feet tall, but he's built more like a racing bike propped up on its rear wheel, like Abe Lincoln fresh out of Springfield. When he was dressed in a navy jacket with brass buttons, though, he looked like a million bucks. He upped the last bid by twenty-five dollars and drove that beast home to Brooklyn, testing the siren along the East River Drive.

After replacing the transmission, Moses and our mutual friend
Susana traveled in the station wagon to Cancún in August of 1976,
with a surprise for me in the back—the bold yellow-and-red-print
upholstered sofa from Bloomingdale's that my Aunt Eileen had left
me. Moses got it across the border by convincing the customs
agents that he was bringing it to Mexico to have it reupholstered in
leather.

During that visit we pored over the map, hoping to locate
every *cenote* we had heard about, and every beach at the end of an
unpaved road.

"Look," I pointed out, "check out this long, narrow island on
the north coast. I wonder what it's like…"

We chose a Sunday to drive to the little mainland port facing
the island.

This was a weekend when the papers had announced there
would be no electricity in Cancún because of an overhaul of the
generators. There were only one or two tiny towns on the road
west. After an hour we turned north onto a lesser road,
pockmarked with potholes. Here it was important to keep an eye
out for turkeys, pigs and barefoot children. The houses along the
way had roofs thatched with palm leaves. In front yards grew thick
bushes of the same palms, long-leafed *guano* or the smaller *chi'it*.
Each homeowner was producing his own roofing material. Pointy-
leafed papaya trees had fruits that looked like long breasts hanging
from the trunks. Between the hamlets we passed cornfields, some
with enormous trees standing alone amid the stalks, gigantic ceibas
and monkey-ear trees.

At last the road came to an end at the water's edge.

A few cars were parked near the wooden ferry landing, a few
stick-walled palapas lined the beach, but there was no ferry in sight.
After we parked the car, we walked up some shaky steps to a
second-story palapa bar where we could look out over the water
while we drank a beer and ate some *botana*.

La botana was a grand custom: along with each bottle of beer,
the waiter would bring a small, flat dish nearly overflowing with a
salty local specialty—spotted eagle ray sautéed with tomato, onion

and chile, ceviche of conch with saltine crackers or empanadas of grouper. There was also the casserole of baby shark in tomato-chile sauce baked between layers of fresh tortillas, a sort of *yucateco* lasagna. *La botana* made it impossible to turn the waiter down each time he returned to ask, *"¿Otra?"*

From where we sat we could see that nothing was happening at the pier. Would we sit there drinking Coronas and eating *botana* until sunset? I called out in Spanish to the other table, where some fishermen were enjoying their *chelas* (the local nickname for cold ones), "What time will the ferry leave for the island?"

Now they knew they had a live one on the line. "The ferry will leave," one answered me, "as soon as Don Anselmo gets here."

"Ah," I answered, "and what time will Don Anselmo get here?"

"When it's time for the ferry!"

Peals of laughter filled the little bar.

A few of the men came to our table to make friends. They asked me if I would like to have a black girl.

"What?" I took the bait.

"Yes, maybe you and your friend here would each like to have a black girl."

Shortly, a tray appeared with two black ones—*dos negras, cervezas negras*, that is. The brand name is Cerveza Leon Negra, and they're really good on an afternoon when you're horsing around with some fishermen and waiting for the ferry. Which appeared as soon as we'd finished our *negras* and paid up. The fishermen wished us, *"Que les vaya bien,"* that it should go well for us, and said that there would be more *negras* waiting when we came back.

The smooth ride over still waters was exquisite in the changing colors of the late afternoon. After sunset the sky and the whole watery world turned deep pink. Even the sand was pink and silent as we approached the island's leeward inlet. But before the boat docked, a whirlwind of boyish noise came careening our way.

"Taxi, TAXI!!!" we heard in a chorus of youthful voices. Racing toward us was the ancient chassis of a big, old car, with six or seven wild-haired urchins hanging onto a kind of raft they had nailed together atop it, one standing and steering, the rest running as fast as they could behind it, propelling the old hunk of junk.

"TAXI!" We climbed aboard.

But then they wanted to know where we wanted to go, and we had no idea.

The boys talked it over and decided to take us to the park. Up a sandy avenue they pushed us, until we reached the plaza at the center of town. It was alive with kids at play. Older people stood on the fringes of the plaza, laughing together and smoking cigarettes.

There we stood a short while, watching the *lotería* games, the basketball, the kids on swings and fishnet climbing structures. Soon a nice-looking teenager came up and asked where we were from, whether we wanted a place to stay the night, and if we wanted a little something to smoke. We did.

Our guide led us to a small cinderblock house next to the water. It was dark now, but gas lanterns illuminated the palapa ceiling, the cots, the fishing nets and rifles hanging on the whitewashed walls.

"What's with the rifles?" I asked the fellow who had just rolled a massive joint, a *"chu-bee,"* he called it. He inhaled deeply. "We're the coast guard," he explained. A little while later I started feeling terribly hungry, and suggested we go out to find something to eat. The coast guard took another deep toke. "I can't go," he said in a tight voice, trying not to exhale any of the smoke in his lungs, "I'm on duty."

"This island," Moses said to me, raising his eyebrows high, "is the place we've been looking for."

23 *Equinox at Chichén Itzá*

March 21st, the day of the vernal equinox, is a national holiday too. It is the birthday of Mexico's most beloved president, Benito Juárez. It is also one of two days in the year when afternoon sunlight allows Chichén Itzá's Pyramid of Kukulkán to perform its renowned light-and-shadow show.

One spring my tour-guide friends Carolina and Hilda decided I needed to be there with them to witness this marvel. In addition, they wanted me to critique the language of their tours.

"The Mayan pyramid known as El Castillo," Hilda began in a practiced tone, "with its square temple at the top, is one hundred feet tall, like a ten-stories building. Its four-cornered base is over one hundred eighty feet wide on each side, as long as three Olympic swimming pools. It was constructed more than thirteen hundreds years ago."

"*¡Fíjate que chingones eran!*" Hilda added, "Just think what advanced motherfuckers they were!"

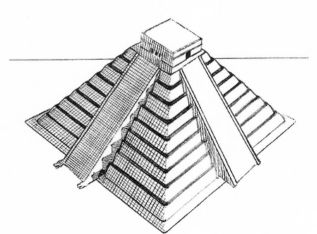

I made note of her extra s's.

Tall, dark-haired Carolina and tiny blonde Hilda had walked into my school one evening a few years earlier with a request. Hilda, speaking beautiful English with only minor mistakes, asked if I could write a letter on Escuela Xicalango stationery to confirm for the tour guide union that Carolina spoke English.

"How long did you study English?" I asked Carolina. She shook her head.

"No estudié ni madres," she laughed. "Are you kidding? I don't need it— I'm only going to give tours in Spanish."

But before Caro left that night, Hilda and I had coerced her into enrolling in a Level 1 class. She kept at it, enlivening one class after another through Level 5, by which time her English was nearly as fast and funny as her Spanish. She proved that Mexico City slang can translate perfectly. Her enthusiasm splattered everyone around her, like water shaken from a puppy's back. She was wild about the Mayans, about her career as a tour guide, and about her life with Hilda.

Around this time I was going out with a doctor, or maybe it was a diver—or a chef. Anyway, with none of them did I have what Caro and Hilda had, together in the ruins, or in their tidy apartment with the sleeping alcove curtained in crystal beads.

"And on the fall and spring equinox," Carolina proclaimed, "this gigantic es-truct-ture does a magic trick, and we're gonna see it in a minute!"

I was getting a free tour, but it was not exactly a private tour. Tourists overheard the guides' speeches, and tried to pass themselves off as part of our "group." Kids pressed around us too; hundreds of local schools bus their students to Chichén Itzá on Benito Juárez's birthday to see the Feathered Serpent slither to earth. Dance troupes performed the *jarana*, the typical dance of the peninsula, accompanied by brass bands. The women looked gorgeous in their lacy embroidered *terno* dresses, roses tucked behind their ears; the men were sharp in white Panama hats and starched white *guayaberas* and slacks.

As usual, the rivalry between Central Mexico and the Peninsula stuck a middle finger into the event; while *yucatecos* danced to *jarana* melodies, *altiplano* ensembles turned up the volume on giant boom boxes so that their dancers could flounce ruffled skirts and stomp their heels to *"¡Guadalajara, Guadalajara!"*

You wouldn't expect the pre-Columbian faction to stay at home on a day like this, would you? Dressed only in breechcloths and feathered headdresses, copper-colored chests and haunches gleaming, young men bellowed deep tones through conch shell trumpets, beat on drums and shook shakers. I was fascinated with the athletic dancers, but Caro and Hilda barely gave them a glance.

"On the vernal equinox," Caro gestured with her long, slim arms, "when the setting sun touches the nine tiers of the pyramid on its western side, it casts their shadows on the side of the stairway." After sunset was when Caro's day *really* began. She had taught me the meaning of the Mexican term *sonsacar:* to awaken a friend in the middle of the night and drag her someplace where the music is really happening, or to a distant pier to watch a meteor shower. None of us had phones yet—Caro would just come to my house and throw pebbles at my window.

Ladylike Hilda, a third-generation German-Mexican who was often mistaken for a tourist, surprised people when they heard her florid Mexico City expressions, her *calo*. She continued the tour:

"That stairway runs from the rattlesnake's open jaws at the foot of the pyramid, all the way up to the summit, where the priests gave the victims their sacrificial *putazos*. The zig-zag shadow is the body of Kukulkán, the feathered serpent god who descends from the heavens to rule the Mayan people. And that includes you, Déborah." Hilda and Caro liked to kid me about the time I carried my snorkeling gear with a tumpline on my head, like a Mayan construction worker. And they imitated my *yucateco*-New York accent whenever they got the chance.

Caro took up the narrative again in her *capitolino* accent: "So on the EE-qui-nox, when the setting sun shines on the pyramid, it is an es-TRORR-di-nary sight!"

"But," I noted, "when the sun won't come out, that pile of stones is about as exciting as a TUM," (I rhymed the word for a burial chamber with "rum," which is how Hilda always said it.)

This particular first afternoon of spring, the sky was a uniform gray, with a curtain of low clouds hovering above the horizon and no sun in sight. The thousands of visitors milled aimlessly. Hawkers hawked corn on the cob and Mexican blankets. Babies cried, girls and boys flirted. People wandered the path to the Observatory in the area known as Old Chichén, built in the elaborate Pu'uc style of architecture. Dispiritedly they ambled toward the Sacred Cenote, dropping pieces of popcorn for racquet-tailed mot-mot birds to fight over.

Until suddenly, the sun emerged below the clouds! A mad dash began from all directions, the whole crowd rushing toward the Great Pyramid, to see that serpent slither.

"*¡Córrele, Déborah, run!*" Caro shouted, "We're gonna get to see it!"

Thousands dashed pell-mell down rocky paths. Many jumped from the Platform of Venus, from the steps of the Observatory. Others emerged abruptly from the Temple of the Phalluses, a personal favorite of mine. They were dropping cameras, pushing, jostling. The kind of people who usually dawdle across the street against the light were now hot-footing it. The hyperacoustics of the Ball Court rang with the racket.

And then the sun slipped behind another layer of clouds.

"*¡Chinga su madre!*" some swore, while others shook their fists, shouting "*¡No te me escondes, serpiente!* Don't you go hiding on me, you snake!" Everyone turned away again, laughing at everyone else for how silly they had looked, running for nothing. People headed back toward the souvenir stands, back to the cold-drink vendors. We caught our breath and the pace slowed once more.

Until the sun snuck out again. This time we were standing on the Platform of the Tzompantli, with its hundreds of gray skulls carved on the sides. By sheer good luck, from this vantage point we had a clear view of the sacred serpent. The multitudes stampeded anew toward the Great Pyramid, but we stood still in awe. We saw the god Kukulkán undulating from sky to earth, from the top of the pyramid to his open jaws on the ground. Caro put one long arm around Hilda and the other around me, and the three of us gazed at the pyramid, dazzled by the wonder our Mayan ancestors had created.

24 The Cave of the Sleeping Shark

I had a friend from Germany named Astrid who lived with her boyfriend on Isla Mujeres. She usually visited me Wednesdays, when she did her marketing in Cancún. One visit began with an invitation for me to join her and a few tourists the coming Sunday on a trip to the Cave of the Sleeping Sharks. Her boyfriend Pepe would lead the dive. I'm sure I responded,

"¡Cómo no!"

Everyone talked about sharks in Cancún and Isla Mujeres—I think it was the favorite subject, after food and the opposite sex. I'd heard about the cave and I'd read about it in *National Geographic*. The article was by marine biologist Eugenie Clark, a City College friend of my Uncle Arturo. In the article there was a photo of a child hitting a huge shark on the nose with a clipboard. The caption identified the child as Clark's daughter Aya, 13. She was taking notes on an underwater clipboard when the shark attacked her. Clark added that Aya's action had routed the gigantic animal. She warned readers to never enter such a dangerous situation without a clipboard.

This cave was discovered in the nineteen sixties by an Isla Mujeres lobsterman. Previously it was thought that sharks are always on the move; scientists had believed that sharks always needed to stay moving to keep an adequate supply of oxygen passing through their gills. But there are strong currents around these caves, and fresh water seeps in from mineral springs beneath the ocean floor. This combination of factors apparently makes it possible for sharks to just "hang out."

I slept, or tried to sleep, at Astrid and Pepe's place in Isla Mujeres's colonia on Saturday night. Pepe kept telling stories late into the night to people who drifted in and out. He was playing the guitar and singing, *";Ay, que bonito es volar!"* from the many-versed ballad of La Bruja. It seemed I should still be asleep, but Astrid wished me a bright "Good morning!" and handed me a mug of coffee. The sky was getting light, and soon we were at the *lancheros'* dock on the bay of *Mujeres*, greeting the tourists.

Pepe and two other men stocked the motorboat with tortas, a cooler of beer and *refrescos* (sodas), and all the tanks, weights, vests and regulators needed for six divers on a single dive.

The motorboat took off toward the north, passing Playa del Norte and the long pier. We continued in a northeasterly direction for a good while. The Americans napped while Astrid and I chatted. Her plan was to sketch birds and watch from above while we dove, because her sensitive ears didn't allow her to dive below the surface. I looked back past our wake and saw the thin line that was Isla Mujeres disappear. On we motored. Sometimes the man at the bow would look back at Pepe at the helm—a bit more toward the north, he would signal, moving his hand up and down.

"How does he know?" I wondered. Astrid shrugged her shoulders. Pepe answered me like a Jewish grandfather, with another question:

"How do *you* know what to teach people in English? He knows." he said. "He knows."

As a teenager in Ensenada, Pepe had become fluent in English by watching American TV stations. He sounded like a TV, in fact, amusing patter segueing into song, back to a joke, then a warning.

"Be careful of the sharks," he told a nervous young woman from Nebraska, *"Ten cuidado con los tiburones."* As if they were puddles to step over.

Pepe had a round brown face, thick brown arms and legs, and tousled wavy hair, sunburned blond. His beer belly poked out the bottom of his florid Isla Mujeres tee shirt. On the shirt, a multicolored sun was setting into its reflection in a turquoise sea.

The lower curve of his belly completed the circle of the sun. One of the women asked him where he had gotten that marvelous shirt.

"Painted it myself," he smiled, winking at me. Astrid had painted it, and hundreds more, signing them with Pepe's initials. She had no working papers, and could have been deported for selling her own artwork.

At the helm of the motorboat, with the lovely Astrid at his side and the tourists and me looking to him as our guide, Pepe was in his element. *"¡San Marqueña de mi vida!"* he belted out the risqué lyrics over the drone of the motor.

About half an hour after our last sight of land, the *lanchero* at the bow turned and said, *"Aquí es."* This is the place. To me, it was a navigational miracle.

We weighed anchor, and everyone looked over the side. Clear water revealed yellowish reefs sixty or seventy feet below. We prepared for the dive, and then, one by one, we propelled ourselves backwards over the side and into the water, as divers are instructed to do.

Clear water. Cool, cold, plenty of current. It was important to stay together. On the ocean floor, I could now see that we were about to enter a series of interconnected caves. The light was dim. Pepe led the five tense divers from one cave to another.

The first cave was wide, sandy and empty. Through a rocky opening we entered the second, to find four sharks in a wavering ring. Caribbean reef sharks, I guessed, which have been known to attack divers. Was that the kind of shark that had gone for Eugenie's daughter? Their tails swayed slightly. Were they sleeping? I had seen a shark while diving once before—it had made my knees turn to flan. But these were dozing. And there were six of us. And Pepe, our dive-master, was with us. We were fine, right?

One of the sharks was much smaller than the others. Three were adults, seven or eight or nine feet in length. Their tiny eyes were open, but of course they were asleep. Their underslung jaws hung open. They have seven rows of teeth, sharks do, and the serrated ivory blades are hinged to move up and down, in and out, to find the right angle of attack.

We five divers huddled to one side of the ring of sharks, while
Pepe swam inside. The small shark was just a baby, only three or
four feet in length. Beer-bellied Pepe swam around the baby, then
behind it, and posed there for one tourist's underwater camera. He
put his arms beneath the little gray torpedo. Was he really going to
touch it? He was—he cradled it. Rock-a-bye, baby, he
pantomimed, and…Baby woke up! Away from Pepe he sped, and
brushed against the daddy shark in his retreat. Big Daddy blasted
out of the circle—then they all caromed off each other, and
screamed out of the enclosure like giant bats.

Flan, I said my knees had felt like once before. Now it was not
just the knees, the feeling that started at my ankles and extended up
to my throat. And it wasn't flan, it was more a sort of watery peach
Jell-O that my internal organs had turned into. Jell-O on the platter
of a laughing man. In fact, we were all laughing into our dive masks
and regulators. Hysterical, laughing blobs of Jell-O.

We returned to the surface, hitched ourselves back up into the
lancha, and motored toward Isla Mujeres, emitting huge sighs of
relief, punctuated by more fits of hysterical laughter and sarcastic
remarks about Pepe
and his prank.

"What did you
want?" Pepe
answered with glee,
"You didn't want
to see the sharks
just *sleeping*, did
you?"

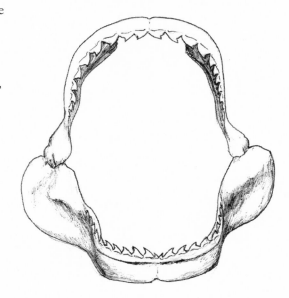

25 *Janet and the Dolphins*

Laughing, Janet entered the school for the first time; she had been joking about mosquitoes with some students outside the door. I overheard bits of the conversation through the screen door, a competition about whose legs had a greater number of mosquitoes. Janet must have been the winner, because her legs were so much longer and broader than anyone else's. She was a handsome blonde, nearly six feet tall, with the muscles of an athlete.

The joking had been in Spanish, and Janet continued in *castillano*, as people called the language of Mexico, when she came inside. Addressing me formally, Janet told me that she was interested in teaching at Xicalango, and that she had just graduated from the University of Texas at Austin with a dual major in Spanish and education. I asked in Spanish whether she spoke English too, and we had a good laugh. She was only about twenty, but I felt sure that she would make an excellent teacher.

The students took to her right away, and she was a great asset during Social Fridays, with her strong voice and dramatic pantomimes of new vocabulary from the songs. After her first term was over, her students asked that Janet teach their second course, and then their third. Many finished their studies at Escuela Xicalango having had only one teacher over a period of more than a year, only Janet.

Along with Ronnie, another great young teacher out of University of Texas at Austin, Janet introduced me to windsurfing and sailing little Sunfish sailboats. Like running, this was an activity we could fit between our morning and evening classes. It didn't take long to get the knack of handling a Sunfish; Janet and I would each rent one at the pier at Hotel Bojorquez, and off we would sail, the only vessels on the whole bay of Mujeres.

With one good breeze, a Sunfish could sail far out into the bay, to where the hotels looked like so many cubes of sugar along the shore. Out there, not a sound could be heard but the luffing of the sail and the riffle of the boat through the water. Close to the beach the bottom was covered in turtle grass; farther out, where the bottom was clear, you could appreciate how transparent the water was. The noonday sun cast shifting, interlocking rainbow patterns on the white sand below. Janet and I sailed alongside each other, pointing out starfish on the seafloor or cormorants diving just ahead. But what I saw all at once emerging from the water wasn't a cormorant's wing—it was a dolphin's dorsal fin, and then the tail, as it spooned in and out of the water.

A second dolphin appeared between our two Sunfish, and shortly we realized we were in the middle of a pod of dolphins, five or six or seven, not much smaller than our own vessels, and content at including us in their school.

The dolphins stayed close by, adjusting their speed to ours. There were two to my right, then one just in front of Janet, and another between us, his forehead gleaming, his grin visible beneath his bottle nose. I called to Janet, "Here he is," but gently, because we were so close we didn't need to use much volume. I wanted to make no more noise than the dolphins were making. Janet pointed out another one, much smaller, a baby dolphin trailing behind us. We sailed, they escorted us, we tacked, they turned, we slowed down, and so did they, with their tender smooth grey backs and their round blowholes.

Finally one of the dolphins must have guessed that we would make an appreciative audience. Eight feet long and over one thousand pounds in weight, the animal propelled his bulk into the air, and balanced a moment on his tail, dancing for us. What could we do but applaud and cheer? As he sank back into the water, we could see his eyes turning from one of us to the other. And then he jumped up again and performed an encore. We screamed with laughter and delight.

Back to shore we sailed together, in joyful awe.

Around then Janet began swimming in the *Día de la Marina* (Navy Day) competitions, and winning them. If she could compete in more than one category on the same day, she might win in each. I heard that some marines were grumbling that she shouldn't be allowed to compete, because she was a woman, or maybe because she didn't smoke; anyway, they said, it wasn't fair!

In the coming years, Janet began windsurfing the six miles to Isla Mujeres. On occasion she swam there, too.

One year for her birthday celebration, Janet invited me on an excursion on a yacht that her student Eduardo was in charge of. That morning on our way to the pier, Janet surprised me with the news that this Eduardo, a small, serious young man from Mexico City, was her boyfriend. Once we arrived, she introduced me to Eduardo's friend Manolo. Snorkeling alongside Manolo at Punta Nizuc, watching him spear a lobster and prepare it for us, I thought Eduardo looked puny and inexperienced at Manolo's side. I liked that Manolo.

The next Social Friday while everyone else was singing, I noticed Eduardo watching Janet with a weird intensity. She appeared totally comfortable as a teacher, relating to all the students and the other teachers. The more relaxed she seemed, the stiffer he became.

Janet told me how difficult Eduardo's childhood had been. Later she related how the police in Cancún had water-boarded him on a false charge. There were a million reasons to feel sorry for him, and she loved him, she said. And so they married, and she got pregnant, or vice-versa.

Janet taught English, swam and windsurfed through that pregnancy. In fact, she was still windsurfing in her eighth month; on her tall, strong frame, that baby bump was merely that, a bump. Shortly before the baby was due, she gave me notice, and she and her husband left together for Texas. Her last name is one of the most common in the US, and his last name is equally common in

Mexico, and in Texas too, I guess. I wish I knew where Janet might
be now. I hope she's in the water.

26 Getting to Know Manolo

During Janet's birthday excursion, Manolo reminded me that we had met once before, at an Escuela Xicalango Halloween Party. He said that I had given him a prize for his costume, and that along with the prize I gave him a kiss.

Then I remembered: he was very convincing as a pirate. Later I learned that he was a descendant of pirates, like many people of the Yucatán coast. That night I had admired his thick, sunburned blond-and-brown hair, and his buccaneer's hat with the flamingo feather for a plume. A life-sized paper maché parrot was perched on one broad shoulder, and a silver dagger flashed at his waist. He wore a black eye patch; the other large brown eye watched me intently.

Halloween is not a Mexican custom, but elaborate homemade costumes have long been *de riguer* in Mexico, for *Carnaval, for Día de la Virgen de Guadalupe,* for Three Kings' Day and other holidays. The Mexican gift for folk art, I believe, stems from the continual fabrication of costumes, masks, altars, floats and other festival decorations. Manolo could whip up a fantastic disguise in minutes.

Creativity and fine handiwork were two of Manolo's many strengths. Shortly after we met, he surprised me with a little scuba diver he had carved out of tortoise shell, for me to wear on a chain around my neck. It was a marvel of grace and precision. There was even a tiny silver wire to represent the air hose from the diver's tank to his mouthpiece. I watched in the mirror as Manolo closed the clasp, imagining tiny air bubbles rising from the little diver's mouth.

One afternoon soon after Janet's birthday, as Manolo walked me home from lunch at his aunt's house, we passed a shapely *flor de mayo tree*. In Hawaii they call it frangipani. The creamy white petals of the flower fan out in a spiral, each petal edged with dark red and bright, hot yellow. Chanel chose this scent for her divine perfume No. 9. Its aroma intoxicates, slows your step, makes you sigh.

"That's my favorite flower," I told Manolo. He released my hand and walked over to the tree, an element in the landscaping of a small hotel's garden. "He's going to pick me one," I thought, watching him size up the tree and its location. But instead, Manolo grasped a green branch from which grew three or four smaller branches tipped with flowers, and simply snapped it off. White milk flowed from the broken limb in Manolo's brown hand.

I looked around; no one was watching. Back at my house, Manolo half filled a large glass with water and put the broken end of the green branch into it. The flowers were still there the next day, and the day after. New buds opened. Its warm perfume enhanced my days.

Manolo examined the broken end of the branch every time he returned to see me. He asked me to give it fresh water when he couldn't. After a week he pointed out small, fuzzy buds at the base and sides of the branch. They grew into white shoots. Within two weeks they were rudimentary roots.

Then Manolo dug a deep hole not far from the front steps.

"How deep are you digging?" I asked, a little put out by his presumptuousness.

"Deep enough," he smiled into the hole without a pause in his digging. Large stones went into the bottom of the hole for good drainage, then smaller ones. He planted the branch carefully, making a little furrow around the hole. I held the branch straight while he filled the space around it with moist soil.

The *flor de mayo* took root. The flowers fell off, but emerald-colored leaves appeared, furled like little umbrellas. The branches elongated, swelled, and grew. It was raining regularly, northerly storms, followed by days of drizzle and drip. Afternoons the sun emerged low on the horizon, and steam rose from the sidewalks, *bochorno* they call it. Fresh downpours followed in the evening. Between rains, the leaves unfurled, and more branches appeared.

When I met him, Manolo was working as a fishing technologist for the Department of Fish and Game. This job kept him on the road more than half the time. Because the people of the island had been fishing *escama*, fish with scales, for generations, they were equipped to teach "the four arts of fishing," a wide variety of techniques, to people in the new fishing communities. Practically nothing was being harvested in those new towns besides lobster and conch. In Punta Allen and Mahajual, conch was now off limits nearly all year, and lobster were on their way to being fished out. It was an important job Manolo and his teammates were doing.

The teammates came from coastal areas throughout southern Mexico, and they and their girlfriends were fun to hang out with. Manolo was the artist of the team, among other responsibilities; he was illustrating the manual they were putting out for the fishing communities.

His schedule was good, as far as I was concerned. When I was busy with the school he was away, but we could enjoy weekends together.

I was thirty-three, Manolo, twenty-one. I was the owner of a successful language school, and everyone knew me as *La Maestra*. Manolo lived at his aunt's house when he was in Cancún, one of half a dozen island cousins sleeping in hammocks in her living room. I was earning enough with the school that I never had to think about money. He was living on a meager government salary. I had a master's degree in teaching ESL, and I liked to write stories. Manolo would write me little notes, lovely little notes, with every other word misspelled. He had nearly completed fourth grade, he told me, when his parents decided he should help his grandfather on his fishing boat. He had five younger brothers and sisters, after all.

One morning I arose from my hammock and looked back at sleeping Manolo. Even asleep, the muscles in his tanned arms and chest looked vigorous. One leg folded down out of the hammock, the foot touching the tile floor. It was a slim leg, but the calf looked strong. His foot was wide at the toes. He liked to stand at the helm of a boat and steer with his foot, his toes grasping or just maneuvering the tiller. This was a tough young fisherman's foot.

In sleep, he had the same expression I had seen when he was listening to people—trusting, engaged. He was lying in the "hammock for three" I had bought in my first weeks in Cancún. It looked vibrant behind Manolo. Manolo looked sculptural in it. Regardless of how different we were, I wanted that young man in my hammock every chance we got.

I thought about Diana and Prince Charles, who were courting at the time. There was a difference of twelve years between them too, and look how happy they were! And the *flor de mayo* was flourishing. Soon it came into luscious, fragrant bloom.

 *27* *International Women's Club Play-on-Words*

Lorraine, a popular Xicalango teacher who became my good friend, invited me to join the International Women's Club. I said to myself, if a woman like Lorraine finds this club worth joining, then I'm going to look into it. Lorraine had come to Cancún with her *acapulqueño* husband and her Iowa farm skills, which she put to work by making and selling cookies and cakes, and sewing clever stuffed animals.

In fact, although most of the club members were in Cancún because they had married Mexicans, the similarity ended there, and the club was a diverse and lively group. We held fashion shows, benefits and lunches for a day school for kids with disabilities, and once we put on a play, a series of skits about the language misunderstandings we had all experienced.

* * *

Laurie's story concerned a visit to the butcher. "I had no idea why," she drawled, and her "why" seemed to stretch all the way to Tennessee, "why that butcher was starin' at me laik that. I was just askin' for a couple of chicken breasts," she declared. *"Chichis de pollo.* Isn't that how you say it?"

"Chicken tits" is what she had requested.

* * *

Melinda had a story about a group of people who entered a restaurant and were greeted in smooth, courteous English by the hostess. "Good evening. How many are you? Would you kindly follow me? May I seat you in this booth? Your waiter will be with you in a moment." The women complimented the hostess on her excellent English, and her nod and smile seemed so genuine. After they had all had a few minutes to look at their menus, one member of the group turned quite pale and shaky. While Melinda was fanning her and the others were trying to attend to her, she slipped off her banquette and onto the floor.

Melinda got up and said to the hostess, "My friend is sick. She fell on the floor and we need some help to get her outside."

Señorita Hostess replied in her gracious way, "Good evening, how many are you? Would you kindly follow meee…"

* * *

At the cash register in a small supermarket with her new boyfriend, Nora asked him if he had any change. The cashier didn't have change for a two-hundred-peso bill, and she hoped her friend would have it. "Are you carrying any cash?" she wanted to ask.

"Traes algo de efectivo?"

He blushed before cracking up.

"You asked me," he whispered, "if anything of mine is defective."

* * *

Jennifer's story was about a voluptuous friend of hers who had studied Spanish before coming to Cancún for a visit. On the beach she wore a diminutive red-and-white bikini on her lovely, full figure, with little string bows securing the bottom part.

One afternoon a young man the friend met on the beach seemed overwhelmed with the little bows; while he talked to her, he kept pulling at the ends of a bow, and of course it came open. She understood none of what he was saying, and apparently he didn't understand what she said either. As she feverishly retied the bow, she yelled *"¡Vámonos, vámonos!"* which she thought meant "Go away!" The guy was probably suggesting some private places they might visit, since *"¡Vámonos!"* means "Let's go!" Sometimes a little Spanish is worse than none at all.

* * *

Early in my stay in Cancún, while I was out of town for a weekend, someone broke in through the wooden louvers of a front window. The thieves got my typewriter, my sewing machine, jewelry my mother had left me, and more.

I was incensed. It hadn't occurred to me that wooden louvers, so common in the tropics, were so vulnerable. I filed a police report at the station house as soon as I had listed the missing items.

The policemen were sympathetic, and assured me that the next day they would send over a little dog. *"Enviarémos un perrito,"* they said.

"Why a *perrito?"* I asked angrily. "If you want to help me, send a BIG dog, not a puppy!" Why did this leave them in a state of hysteria, when I was serious? How dare they send a little puppy!

But what they were intending to send was not a *perrito*—it was a *"perito,"* an expert, a fingerprint expert, that is. They were still doubled over as I left the station.

* * *

The "line" to check in at the airport resembled those shifting schools of silvery fish at Isla Mujeres' Garrafon—an amorphous blob of individuals bulging out to one side, then the other. Who was next? Who would miss their flight? Who knew? But it certainly would NOT be the tall, apparently gay gentleman with the large pink-and-black-plaid rolling suitcase. He was wedging his rounded hips between couples, separating mothers from children as he made his way to the counter. With each bold step his husky whisper implored permission to pass through the crowd. His way of begging pardon was pronounced, "Squeeze me, squeeze me, please, squeeze me!"

* * *

I sat at the counter at a posada, a lunch place in the market in Valladolid, listening carefully as the waitress reeled off the names of the specials of the day. I tried not to notice all the curious Mayan eyes staring at me.

Sopa de lima, the waitress said,
and *Pollo en escabeche,*
Carne adobado,
Costillas de puerco,
Carne asada and

Longaniza con huevo.

The others dining there didn't turn their heads toward me, but I had the feeling that everyone put off chewing, the better to hear if the *ch'ela* (Mayan for "light one") could speak Spanish, and what she would order. At times like this my Spanish always fell to pieces.

But I mustered all the confidence I could, and requested the *"cosquillas de puerco."* So why were all those brown faces turning red and looking everywhere but at me? And why was the waitress stiffening her mouth, trying not to explode? I had just ordered the pork ribs, *¿que no?* Well, no, what I had ordered was the "tickles of pork!"

The International Women's Club skit brought down the house.

 *"¡Como Perro!"*

La Manzana 3, home of Escuela Xicalango, at the junction of Avenues Uxmal and Nader, was one of Cancún's best addresses in the 'seventies. *Manzana 23, Manzana 28*—these were working-class neighborhoods with little houses of cinderblock built on small rectangular plots of land. The houses in *Manzana 3,* though not necessarily luxurious, were larger than those of the other *manzanas* and were built on larger plots. Many were two or three levels, with attractive landscaping and ornate front gates.

My neighbors in the *Manzana 3* were FONATUR officials, city officials, doctors, business owners and hotel managers. Many homes had high walls around their gardens and metal gates you couldn't see through. Walls and fences like these were very common; some had broken bottles topping the high walls.

One afternoon as I was returning home, I noticed a cordon of police cars in front of a neighbor's home. Actually, it was more like a pile-up—there must have been twenty or thirty police vehicles. They were parked all across the street like odd puzzle pieces, blocking traffic. I knew the family whose house was surrounded, but not so intimately that I wanted to knock on their door to ask what was the matter. Nor did I wish to ask anything of the policemen, sitting alert in their cars, talking on their radios.

So I entered the school and dismissed the matter from my mind.

The next morning the radio broadcast news about a disaster that would affect nearly every Mexican. President Lopez Portillo, soon to end his six-year term of office, had announced a seventy percent devaluation of the Mexican peso.

The World Bank had been calling for this. In the mid-
'seventies Mexico had enjoyed a few boom years, when the price of
oil was high and the peso was sound. Then, the fall of the price of
oil, coupled with extravagant government borrowing and spending,
had destabilized the Mexican economy. It was not surprising that
the value of the peso fell. But the timing of the event came as a
surprise to nearly everyone.

It meant that if you had one thousand pesos under your
mattress and you lived in a place where a great deal of what you ate
and used was imported, those pesos now would buy you three
hundred pesos worth. Businesses stayed closed several hours in the
morning so they could put new price tags on all their merchandise.
Everything imported or that had imported components was
marked up by the afternoon. Throughout Quintana Roo, so far
from the center of Mexico, canned products like powdered milk
and Dutch cheese and ham were a vital part of the diet. National
merchandise took a price hike too.

I've heard that most Mexicans of means had anticipated the
devaluation and deposited their money in foreign banks, in dollars,
of course. But some still had it in Mexico. My neighbor and his
cronies, for example. Apparently he had the muscle to muster a
sizable portion of the police force to keep this private trove safe
and sound. Prior knowledge of the event and its timing had surely
made him and his *compadres* into millionaires.

Only weeks before, when asked about the possibility of
devaluation, President Lopez Portillo had shouted that he "would
defend the value of the peso like a dog!" He shook his jowls as if
tearing into the necks of the peso's detractors. His family
compound, five mansions on a hill outside Mexico City, built
during his term of office, will forever be known as "Dog Hill."

And my neighbor? Greeting everyone with his toothy smile.
One more *perro*.

29 *Xicalango in Jeopardy*

The most important political issue for the school was the immigration status of the teachers. I could hardly ever find Mexicans to fill teaching positions. Nonetheless, it was difficult to get work visas for the *extranjeros*, foreigners, that I hired. Iván, the first teacher I employed, was a *yucateco* who had become fluent studying in Mérida; unfortunately he didn't stay with us for long. Ralph, a Belizean-Mexican, was only sixteen when he started teaching at Xicalango, and he already had a few years of teaching under his belt. Ralph grew up bilingual with his Mexican mom and Scottish dad. He stayed with the school nearly ten years, until he opened his own school. Aside from these two, few Mexicans applied for teaching positions, so I hired the best qualified Americans, Brits, Canadians, Belizeans and others who sought us out.

Across Avenue Nader from the school were the offices of Immigration. While I was in the process of getting my FM2 working permit I had to visit those offices frequently, more nervous each time I crossed their chilly aluminum threshold. Once I had my papers in hand, I did my best to stay off that side of the street.

But immigration came to us, too. Several immigration agents were studying with us, and one would tell me when a sweep of businesses employing foreigners was about to begin. But, he reminded me, it was important to "regularize" the foreign employees as quickly as possible.

This *regularización* was an expensive and time-consuming process, prohibitive unless it seemed that the teacher in question might remain at Xicalango for an extended period.

Sometime around 1980 I realized that I had an excellent and cohesive group of teachers for the more than three hundred students registered. There was Jemima from Michigan, Texans Ronnie and Janet, and Sasha from Long Beach, California. Livewire Danielle from Quebec was teaching French. There was a witty British guy, married to a Mexican woman, and two great-looking single guys, Rick from Missouri and Brad, another Texan. We had hilarious training lunches, with enchiladas to eat and dry Bohemia beer to wash them down, while we played games of "Alibi" and "If," games the teachers and students had a ball with in their classes.

The women teachers liked to go dancing together on weekends. Shortly before midnight we'd gather in my kitchen for one of Danielle's favorite pick-me-ups: a *charro* cocktail, iced black coffee laced with tequila. Then we'd be off to Krakatoa or La Mina to tear it up.

In January, just after the beginning of a winter term, I gathered all the necessary Xicalango documents for each of the teachers, made the requisite triplicate copies, collected their passports, visas and new photos, bought the certified check necessary for each application, and took a briefcase with all of this on the bus with me to Mexico City. Manolo gave me a memorable good-bye kiss at the bus terminal.

I knew quite a bit about *"trámites"* or legal processes by this time, and I felt I could file the papers for the teachers on my own, instead of paying an expensive lawyer a separate high fee for each one. I advised the school secretary that I was staying at the Hotel Edison, facing *El Arca de la Revolución*.

The day that the *trámites* had all been filed and I had bought my ticket for my return bus trip that night, a telegram from Cancún arrived at the Edison: "School closed *(clausurada)* by immigration officials. Students sent home."

That word, *clausurada*, is a frightening one. Sometimes it shows up on a sign in front of a store you've frequented for years; suddenly the doors are taped shut, and the place might never open again.

Meanwhile I had this to think about: we offered students a discount when they paid for a complete three-month course at the beginning of the term. If the school could not reopen quickly, I would owe a refund of several months' tuition to hundreds of students. On top of that, I had already submitted the documents of the seven teachers I was representing in Mexico. That meant they would be without their passports and visas for at least six weeks. With the school closed, I could no longer pay them for teaching, but they could not leave the country either.

Sitting on the edge of my bed in that little hotel room, I looked down at my hands, the right one squeezing the left. My jaws began to ache—I had been grinding my teeth since opening the telegram.

My bus left at seven p.m., and it was only one in the afternoon—what could I do to keep from going crazy until the bus left? I had passed a movie theater that was showing *Superman—The Movie,* the first one starring Christopher Reeve. I decided to leave my bag at reception and go to see the movie, I decided.

Superman sailed over Manhattan, his jaw firm, his gaze clear into the future. He flew purposefully over neighborhoods where I had worked, where I had lived. I could pick out the tennis courts where I used to play in Central Park. Over my very own bridge, the Brooklyn Bridge, I sailed with Superman.

Truly, I do not remember how I managed to resolve the issues and reopen the school. I only remember sitting in the movie theater and knowing I would fly over this crisis.

30 *The Pregnant Bitch*

A well-liked student stumbled through the main door of the school fifteen minutes late for the early morning class. Behind him I heard metal clanging—his bike had fallen as soon as he turned his back on it. He swiveled toward the crashing sound with a pained expression, hesitated, then resumed his march to the front of the classroom. His forehead was wrinkled, and behind his thick glasses, his eyes looked distressed.

None of this was characteristic of Francisco; he was usually punctual, relaxed and easy-going, a slow talker but a fast learner. Now words poured from him in a jumbled stream.

"I've lost my pregnant bitch," he wailed. The class tittered, but he went on. "She's a Dalmatian, a pedigreed Dalmatian named Daisy. She was with me this morning when I went to the store to buy milk at the mini-super at Avenue Chichén Itzá on the corner of Palenque, and when I came out of the store where she always waits for me she was gone…she's going to have her puppies in just a few days and I've never lost her before but I hope all of you can help me find her. She's about this high," he signaled with a flat palm, which Mexicans use only for showing the height of an animal. "She has spots that really look like a daisy on her right side. She answers to Daisy and she must be carrying a lot of puppies because she's very fat!" He demonstrated her girth with two hands.

Francisco paused for breath. "If you find her, I'll give you a puppy!" he promised, looking around the table.

The sixteen adults present leaned forward. Some began asking questions at once. I held up a hand and requested that the questions and answers be in English. Without a pause the students continued, "Where do you live, Francisco? Do you have a telephone? No? Do your neighbors have a telephone? Where do you walk Daisy? How old is she? Can you draw a picture of Daisy? What does she like to eat? What kind of dog is the father of the puppies? Who is your vet?"

We talked about Daisy, and then for the rest of the class we talked about our own dogs and parrots, our tamarin monkeys, our coatimundis and our Yucatán box turtles. We drew them on the board and in our notebooks. We learned dog anatomy, bird behavior, turtle dietary preferences. And Francisco poured out his heart about the canine love of his life. Before he left, he had received more hugs and pats on the back than a soccer champ after the winning goal.

To everyone's delight, the next morning at 7:30, there sat Daisy, next to a bench in front of the school. Reina and her sister Rocio were holding her by the mecate-twine rope looped around her elegant neck. What a fiesta, when Francisco pedaled onto the school patio one moment later and saw his darling! In no time he was down on the pavement on his knees, cheek to snout, embracing her. The students petted Daisy, brought her water, and tried to count the separate forces in her roiling belly. One student said he'd take bets on how many puppies, and how soon. Now we all adored Daisy.

Which was fortunate, because three-and-a-half weeks later Francisco came to the door again, this time just after evening classes had let out, with a dark green backpack full—of puppies! Eleven puppies, wagging. yelping and peeing. He lowered the backpack to the glossy red tile floor. It was the kind of tile made of cement squares, dull when first installed, but shiny now after six years of daily mopping with petroleum. Red tile peppered with white-and-black puppies, running, slipping on their little puddles, snooping about.

"¡Dios mio!" I exclaimed. "And where's Daisy?"

"Home," Francisco moaned. "If we still have a home. My landlady wants to throw us out! 'Twelve dogs!' she says, 'In a one-bedroom apartment? They're out!' she says, 'or you're out!'"

Eleven Dalmatian puppies. Except for the ones who were mostly black. Black with white belly and white collar, white feet and white tail, or the tip of the tail white. Where they were white, they were Dalmatian white, with black spots. Like Dalmatians in black jackets. Or black labs in white socks, with holes in them. Dalmatian. Mix. Puppies.

"I want to give you a puppy," Francisco said, talking fast again. "I'm so grateful to you and the school for finding Daisy for me. Which one do you want? I mean which ones? I wanted to give you one, and give Reina and her sister one, and sell the others, but now that they're not *such* pure Dalmatians, I better give them away. Don't you want three?"

They were cute as ladybugs. They had found the giant tortoise skull that sat on a low shelf in the main classroom and were nosing around it. Through a huge empty eye socket you could see a tiny black-and-white snout. Beneath the blackboard one pup was chewing on an eraser. Another had managed to push open the supply closet door; at any moment, precariously balanced yardsticks and rolled posters were sure to come tumbling out.

A popular song at that time was *"Gavilán o Paloma,"* by José José. The song's protagonist can't decide whether he should swoop in on his lover like a *gavilán*, a hawk, or be gentle like a *paloma*, a dove. As one pup with a black saddle on his back and a white blaze on his forehead pounced on a rubber band ball that had come rolling out of the closet, I thought, *Gavilán*. The ball rolled off to where a second pup had nestled in some student's forgotten sweatshirt. She was the dove, *Paloma*.

From then on, for the rest of my years in Cancún, Gavilán and Paloma were at my side. If not underfoot.

 # *How Old Are You?*

Personal information was the focus of the first half of Book 1: "Where are you from, where are you working, what's your favorite color, what's your favorite food, are you married or single, HOW OLD ARE YOU?" Most students were perfectly content to answer truthfully, "I'm nineteen years old." "I'm twenty-four." Maybe some bumped their ages up by a year or two. The teachers taught the students an optional answer, "I'd rather not say." We practiced, "I'm in my twenties, I'm in my thirties." We laughed at the Mexican joke: "I'm twenty-four—in each foot!"

Not every student was younger than I. There were older married women who deflected that question, just as I tried to do. There were a few older men. Very few, though. Cancún was probably the most youthful town in the nation—young people from all over Mexico were flocking there, meeting the opposite sex and making babies as if they were going out of style. You didn't see much gray hair in this spanking new city. The average age in Cancún was probably under sixteen, and most of the students at Escuela Xicalango were twenty-somethings.

In Spanish the age question is expressed, *"¿Cuantos años tienes?"* which is why Spanish-speaking English learners tend to ask "How many years you have?" or to say, "My boyfriend, he has twenty-one years." Age is such a common subject that I had to hear the same mistake over and over. The only solution was for the students to practice these questions and answers about each other, about famous people, about our brothers and sisters, boyfriends and girlfriends, husbands, wives and children.

That didn't mean that I wanted to answer the question myself. But I insisted on informality. I encouraged students to call me

"Déborah," not Ms. Frisch and not Ms. Déborah. So how could I evade the age question? In every class, people were dying to know how old *la maestra* was. "HOW OLD ARE YOU?" they demanded in unison, like a tragic chorus.

I knew I should never tell them my age. For one thing, I didn't want them to know the difference in ages between me and the boyfriend many had seen me with. I knew I'd catch hell for it.

But in one class after another, once we got to Unit 4, they pushed on Monday, on Tuesday, on Wednesday and Thursday. Finally, in one class I broke down.

"I am thirty-four," I said.

"*¡Dios mío!*" a teenager protested, alarm in her eyes, "my *mother* is thirty-four!" One matron confided that the last of her six children was born when she was thirty-four. Some grandmas in the class were just a smidgen older than thirty-four. Gorgeous grannies they were, too, with long wavy hair and high-heeled sandals. "Thirty-four!" they clucked their tongues. "And unmarried! And no babies!"

My mother had passed away four years before I came to Cancún, so I didn't have maternal pressure on me to get married—instead, I had pressure from a whole school.

In the U.S. I'd had my share of commitment-shy New York boyfriends. I'd gone out with some real players in Mexico, too. Where tourism was the industry, guys who specialized in the four-day visitor were legion. "*Turisteando,*" they called their way of life, dedicated to the tourist trade.

But the first time I kissed Manolo, the man I would marry, he told me that he wanted me to have his son. He never forgot he had told me that. He reminded me in word and deed often, often.

Weeks went by, and he asked me if we had won the lottery this month. Not yet? Maybe next month. Or the next. What a handsome little boy he's going to be, he promised. There was no desperation on Manolo's part, only dedication, to me and his son-to-be. So, more than a year after we started seeing each other, I was very happy to tell him that this month, it seemed we were winners at last.

32 A Little Errand

During the summer before Manolo and I were married, my Swedish friend Britta came to visit. She and I had enjoyed rooming together a few years earlier, during a three-week workshop for ESL teachers in Israel. Long and lanky, with a crooked smile and a boisterous laugh, Britta could make herself comfortable in an unusual setting like Manolo's island, I felt sure. It was the same palmy sandbar on the gulf coast of the Yucatán peninsula that Moses and I had visited years before, the one where we had been greeted by the "taxi."

Around sunrise on our first morning on the island, Manolo stole out of his parents' house at the sound of a low whistle from one of his fishing buddies. Britta and I slept hours longer, then awoke in our hammocks, looking up at the high thatched ceiling. For breakfast we scooped up my future mother-in-law's scrumptious seafood stew with fresh tortillas, and followed it with black beans, an essential part of every meal.

Doña Rosalba, with her short black hair and her shining black eyes, taught us to wash dishes in a wooden washbasin, with a *henekén* brush and one cup of water. The island had no source of fresh water itself—water came through a fifteen-kilometer pipeline from a sweet, pure spring on the mainland. The water flowed for about fifteen minutes, once a day. When it started to pour into the 55-gallon drums, the first to hear it would shout *"¡AGUAS!"* and that call would echo all over town. One member of each family would become vigilant, ready to shut off the faucet before any water spilled onto the sand. Wasting water in a place like this would be a serious mistake.

Evenings, Britta and I walked over to the beach with Manolo and his numerous good-looking cousins. As far as everyone on the island was concerned, I was now related to nearly half of the thousand islanders, and feeling more comfortable there day by day. We drank gin out of coconuts and shot the breeze around a driftwood fire, smoking the Colombian pot that the cousins caught in their fishing nets. Bales of it were sometimes jettisoned by boats or small planes under pursuit. It was said that one islander had forty-two kilos of the stuff buried in the sand.

On the morning before Britta's return to Sweden, the morning we were to leave, my father-in-law Don Leandro offered us a ride to the mainland in his *lancha*. A cigarette dangling from his lips, he said he had a little errand to take care of on the way. His invitation probably sounded like this:

"¿Quierenir nalancha?" He spoke Islander, that is, leave off the last half of each word, mash the remainder thoroughly. Of course we accepted.

The *lanchas* were open fiberglass motorboats, twenty-four feet long and about four-and-a-half feet wide. The floor was made of widely spaced planks, with four benches spanning it. I would kick off my flip-flops into the boat and step cautiously from pier to bobbing boat. Don Leandro steadied my arm with his calloused brown hand as I placed a bare foot on the gunnels.

"Allí suben dos," he chuckled. "Two boarding." I was pregnant with his first grandchild.

Halfway to the mainland port, Don Leandro said it was time to haul in the *palangre*. That's a long, strong line, fifty meters or more, with many short hooked-and-baited lines attached to it. At dawn, fishermen let out the *palangre*, with an anchor on one end and a float on the other. Late in the day they return to see *"qué pegó"* (what had hit). So this was our errand.

Four small cousins had come along for the ride—Milly and Nelly, Delila and Chepi. Manolo and I, Britta, and two of Manolo's adult cousins were bound for Cancún. Don Leandro was at the helm, and Manolo stood at the bouncing bow, holding onto the bowline and signaling to his dad with one hand: a little farther starboard, come up into the wind, watch out for that patch of seaweed ahead that could foul the engine.

A tiny rainstorm passed over us, and the little girls hid halfway under a green tarp, dancing to a saucy song that Delila was singing at the top of her lungs. Nelly, the smallest girl, was only five, but she could really dance. I commented on this to her eight-year-old sister.

"Hmmph!" Milly sniffed *"Pues ¡solo eso hace!* That's all she ever does!"

The float marking my father-in-law's *palangre*, with its scrap of yellow Xicalango tee shirt for a flag, stood out above the choppy grey sea. Manolo turned toward his father, and Don Leandro cut the engine. He took a little drag on his unfiltered Delicado cigarette and began hauling in the line. Haul haul haul, with sinewy muscular arms just like his son's, only wrinkled at the elbow and more scarred. Haul haul haul JUMP! A huge grayish creature flipped over the gunnels and slapped onto the flooring planks between our bare feet, writhing. Now I could see it was *una gata*, a young nurse shark, about six feet in length, pale and pointed, with double dorsal fins and a long tail. I don't know what alarmed me more as it thrashed about, the two weird fangs dangling from its upper jaw or its shiny, beady eyes.

Don Leandro passed the short wooden club to Manolo, who was closer to the shark's broad head.

"La aspirina,"' said Don Leandro with a wink. Manolo aimed a fatal blow just above the youngster's right eye. Whack! Wham! Like Bruce Lee on a two-by-four. The animal's great tail flopped slack to the floor.

Meanwhile Don Leandro turned back to hauling. WHOMP! Another! Just like the other, and just as lively! This one's head was near the helm, so Don Leandro put it out of its anxiety. But what about us? Britta, the little ones and I were laughing hysterically, trying to keep the sharks off our laps, off our feet. The third one hit the second, and rolled onto little Nelly's legs! Her shriek was like a seagull's, rising above the rush and thrum of water and motor.

The sharks began to look like monstrous sardines in a gigantic can, so smooth and silvery side by side. I could feel their raspy skin on my ankles and smell their salty blood. The little girls squeezed between Britta and me, giggling wildly, still dancing. Then came the fourth shark, bigger than the others, and not as quick to take his medicine.

Now Manolo hauled. Britta, tall as any of the men, pulled in the next one, and I got her picture. Fish slime on her tee shirt and goofy, lopsided smile on her face. No one wanted me hauling, but I poured buckets of seawater over bloody hands and feet. Cousin Chac and Cousin Platos had started filleting and flinging entrails to the frigate birds. The long-winged avian pirates fought over them in midair.

Five sharks. Nine. Eleven. Twelve. Twelve nurse sharks, none under five feet. Guts and gore, silver animals and pink and gray meat all over.

After the last one, Manolo pulled up the anchor and we continued toward the mainland port. We hosed off a bit there, then squeezed into the Volkswagen for the drive back to Cancún, all sticky and exhausted.

The next day we stood by the car, packing Britta's things in the trunk before driving her to the airport for her flight to Sweden.

A crooked smile on her lips, she said to me, "I hope you're not thinking of stopping for one of those 'little errands on the way?' "

33 *Our Wedding, Our Providencia*

Our baby was due mid-November. By June I was feeling pretty tense, especially when I walked into the classroom and noticed all eyes on my belly. I wanted to be married. The Mexican *Secretaría de Relaciones Exteriores* had sent me the list of legal requisites for a foreign national to marry a Mexican—it would have taken months. And that damn list incensed me. What made these Mexicans so precious that a foreigner had to jump through burning hoops to marry one? Manolo and I decided to fly to Orlando and get married there.

But first we needed Manolo's birth certificate and proof of military service so that he could get a visa. Time was running out, and with Manolo's obligations and mine, we could only go to the island on a Sunday. We knew the Town Registry, on the second floor of the tiny *Palacio Municipal* on the plaza, would be closed that day, but we had no other choice.

That Sunday morning, to nourish me and her grandbaby-to-be, Manolo's mother insisted on serving me the cheek of the grouper, and the most luscious morsel of grilled lobster tail. After our hearty breakfast, Manolo and I walked together to the *parque* to look for the Town Registrar.

Don Justo, just the man we were looking for, happened to be leaning on the wall of the *Palacio Municipal*. His pitch-black hair framed an ancient mariner's face. After the two men shook hands, Manolo asked if Don Justo could get him copies of his birth certificate and proof of military service. The older man seemed quite willing, Sunday be damned. "How much will I owe you?" Manolo asked.

"Do you have a cigarette?" Don Justo asked. Manolo produced a Raleigh.

"Got a light?" Manolo lit it for him.

"That'll do," Don Justo laughed, and bounded up the stairs.

The day before we left for Florida I noticed that Manolo's arm was red, right around his tattoo. I had noticed this tattoo the day I met him, probably the handiwork of one of his cousins. It was a curvy woman, big hips and long hair, naked as a seabird. But now she had on a bikini! "What happened to your lady-friend?" I asked him.

"Well," Manolo replied, "we'll be married in a few days. I can't have these naked women hanging around."

To fly to Orlando I wore an embroidered Mexican smock, thinking it hid my belly, but soon I realized I hadn't fooled the Mexicana Airlines clerk. With one almond-eyed glance she took in my face, my shape and my husband-to-be. In an instant she had stepped out in front of her counter, taking me in an embrace as close as two pregnant women can manage.

Now I recognized her; she was Carmen, a Belizean friend of one of the teachers. Her maternity outfit was a blue uniform blouse and a man's wide-shouldered Mexicana Airlines jacket over a uniform skirt (she lifted the back of the jacket to show me that the skirt was unzipped in the back). We eyed each other's size and shape.

"Six months?" Carmen asked, dimpling. I nodded.

"Do they tell you it's a boy?" I asked.

"Absolutely," she laughed. DNA testing and sonograms were not in use there yet, but most of us trusted the Mayan indicators anyway: shape and orientation of the baby bump—we were both sure we'd have boys. Carmen suggested we find a Lamaze class together on Manolo's and my return to Cancún.

In Orlando a justice of the peace married us, simply and promptly. To celebrate we went to Disney World. Pirates of the Caribbean—hmmppf! I had just married one! Captain Nemo's Undersea Adventure? What a joke those plastic octopuses were.

Back in Cancún, Manolo and I prepared for our wedding reception. My brother would come, my father, and Margaret, my best friend from the States. Manolo had been socking away lobster in the freezer—there were more than twenty kilos of it there. Quite a few of his relatives arrived several days in advance to help with the preparations and begin the party. An uncle who owned a shrimp boat showed up with a cooler filled with twenty-five kilos of shrimp, the kind as long as a fisherman's hand. A friend provided twenty delicious *pollos en escabeche*. Guests arrived in *lanchas* from Holbox, with big groupers and snappers that they caught by trolling on the way. These they prepared as *tik-in-shik,* split open, slathered in *achiote* sauce, covered with sliced onions, peppers, chiles and tomatoes, and grilled over a barbecue pit that Manolo's family dug that day.

Friends and family carried the white schoolroom tables out onto the lawn behind the school, with the blue nesting classroom chairs to sit on. It had been raining, and the grass was green as limes. Since *flamboyán* trees were blooming all up and down Avenue Nader, we decorated with lush bouquets of the red blossoms, like flaming orchids, on each table. Our garden could not have looked more festive.

The family of Don Isidro, Manolo's uncle, had arrived two days earlier, father, mother and all eleven children. I had a moment's worry about where they would all sleep, but they had brought their own hammocks. By nightfall, hammocks swung in every nook the school and the house provided. As was normal in the Yucatán peninsula, every room had at least two pairs of hammock hooks. The little kids spent the days squirting the garden hose at each other; the big ones dug the cooking pit, shopped, prepared meals, washed up, and toted crates of beer and sodas.

Why was I surprised that the high waist of my wedding dress wouldn't fit me? Fortunately, I had a back-up outfit, a gorgeous white San Antonino dress, embroidered in red, green and yellow at the yoke. It drew attention away from my waist and toward my rosy face. I wore a fiery *flamboyán* blossom behind one ear. An island cousin ironed my dress as if it were spun of gold. Manolo was tanned and charming in a collarless white guayabera, also pressed to perfection. Our friends' Latin jazz combo played while we danced and feasted.

My father wanted me to ask Don Isidro how he managed to remember the names of so many children; trying to find a way to phrase the question delicately, I decided to ask him an entirely different question, rather than make an issue of the size of his family. This lovely wedding party on which we had spent next-to-nothing made it so clear to me: here, family was so much more valuable than money.

* * *

For months Manolo and I had talked about "Debby's Dream," the little prose poem I had written as a model for the students while we were studying Unit 5: "I'm sitting on my sailboat..." it began. Now it could be our sailboat.

As we talked about it, the idea emerged that, with a sailboat, Manolo could take tourists on fishing trips or excursions to Isla Mujeres. His grandfather had been a sail fisherman and had literally taught him the ropes. With the right fishing gear, Manolo would be able to serve the catch of the day to the tourists and make a good living close to home. We'd have the sailboat for our own fun, too.

No sooner had we begun looking for a sailboat than a man we knew in Isla Mujeres offered us his, La Providencia. It was just what we wanted, a medium-sized wooden sloop. Boats like this one were built by hand in Belize in earlier years—she was about thirty years old. She was twenty-nine feet long, with a full set of canvas sails and a Volvo Penta inboard engine. There was a cabin with bunks for four, a head and a little galley for cooking. She was nicely laid out, and if she had not been meticulously cared for, some work could make her shipshape before the tourist season. We were overjoyed, and we bought her with Xicalango earnings on July 19th, my birthday.

We rented dockage at the Bojorquez pier. I made yellow print café curtains for the cabin, and we spent the rest of the summer weekends fishing, working and hanging out on the boat. La Providencia would be our baby's big rocking cradle.

34 *Arturo's Birth*

Lilia, a student of mine, had mentioned that she was a Lamaze teacher. She was one hot ticket, this Lilia, a small, energetic woman from Mérida. Carmen found a third woman to join us, a little less *panzona* (big-bellied) than we were, and we began weekly pilgrimages to the stylish house near Punta Sam where Doña Lilia was our mentor.

We loved our classes. Lilia's stereo played sparkling Mexican instrumentals of guitars and harps while we did yoga on the rug, alongside wide windows overlooking the sea. We practiced Lamaze breathing techniques, puff-puff, sniff-sniff and *relájate*, relax. She served us limeade in fine icy glasses, mint leaves floating on top. Then we talked about what we expected and what we hoped for.

Lilia spoke about our fast-approaching babies as if she already knew them. The mother of three school children, she was about thirty. She seemed older and wiser, though.

"There are no other babies like yours," Lilia said in her songbird voice. "In fact, there will *never* be another baby just like the one you are carrying. At this moment," she continued as we sat at her feet on the rug, "your baby has infinite potential. He or she might become a great musician or teacher or politician or fireman. You will be your baby's most important teacher. No one else will know what your baby will need, only you and your baby's father." She reminded us to think about how we might help these babies grow into the best people they could be. We three mothers-to-be left Punta Sam glowing, week after week.

Manolo was delighted with the name I chose, Arturo, after my uncle, or Leonora in the unlikely case that this pointy belly of mine should be harboring a girl. Arturo Ávila, what an excellent name, he said. This boy would be the family's first Arturo.

One of my students was a doctor, a good-humored young woman with a curly-headed two-year-old of her own. The doctor usually called her daughter *"Comadrita*, little co-mother." It was clear how much fun they were having together. I started regular visits to her office, and chose the small clinic where I would give birth.

Each time I called my father from the telephone office, he sounded more anxious about me. I knew our present form of communication, with the frequent long waits before a phone came available, would be difficult with a newborn. I had applied for a residential phone more than one year earlier. It wasn't simply a matter of applying, either—I had bought several hundred dollars worth of shares in the phone company in order to get on the list for installation.

While Manolo was *tramitando* the permits for our boat, he was still working for the Fishing Department, sometimes in Isla Mujeres or Cozumel, sometimes in Mahajual or Punta Allen. I realized now that I might need help at any moment—I needed that phone! One afternoon Manolo's supervisor came for a visit, to wish me luck and bring me a good-sized grouper from Manolo. While we talked, I touched my belly. To my astonishment I felt four hard little bumps—the baby was pushing his fist against me. It seemed to me I had better do something about that phone right away.

Telmex was a windowless block of a building out past the *Manzana 5*. Alone, dressed in my favorite maternity dress, I walked in and asked to see a supervisor. We shorties, when we are pregnant, we look really pregnant. I felt that my baby preceded me by a couple of feet, and that was just what I wanted for this conversation.

"Necesito un teléfono, I need a telephone," I said to the slack-faced man in charge, touching my belly with one hand. Then I opened the thick file of my TelMex documents, to show him the

contract. He took off at a run to look for someone else to deal with me.

The next morning the phone was installed.

Manolo was home asleep the following night when my labor began around midnight, three weeks early. I hadn't yet tacked the quilted lining to the inside of the wicker *moisés* cradle we had bought for the baby. How could I bring my baby home without the cradle ready? My expression shifted from wide smile to grimace and back to smile again as I sewed, until the cradle was complete. The Municipal Palace clock chimed two. I woke Manolo and he drove me to the little clinic.

My pretty *doctora* didn't answer her pager. The nurses left her one message after another, but nothing happened. Finally they called another ob-gyn, who arrived in a rush. But there was nothing much for him to do once he had determined how far along I was. I kept going with my Lamaze breathing and stayed calm. The nurses wondered what all this puff-puff sniff-sniff was about. They told me I should stop it, but I explained it to them between contractions. I felt very proud of myself, of my ability to remain in control for six hours, ten hours, eighteen hours. I could hear a woman down the hall having a much harder time. Now I understood why it didn't matter too much what you had with you to read, or what music you had planned to listen to—I found the labor all-consuming.

Manolo had brought hard candy for me to suck on, and he put ice chips in my mouth. He massaged my lower back and wiped my sweaty forehead. He was just fine, and I was just fine…until the last moment. With the pain of the last stage of labor overwhelming me, when the doctor ordered me to push again I yelled back, "Couldn't I DIE doing this?"

Before the doctor could respond to my hysteria, Manolo did.

"Skinnier women than you have had babies," he said. I couldn't help but laugh. Arturo was born in the midst of that laughter.

We were so happy. Tiny Arturo was bellowing, kicking legs and throwing arms about. He had black hair and black eyes, long limbs, long feet and everything else he was supposed to have. He was born on the nineteenth—my birthday is also a nineteenth. Manolo and I had both wanted a boy, and here he was. He was three weeks early, but that seemed to be just one more of his brilliant qualities. I can't remember all the reasons why we felt so enormously lucky, but that is how we felt.

We had agreed earlier that Manolo should drive to the island to get his mother after the baby was born, while I got some sleep. Manolo's mother had promised to stay with us and help us at first. The fact was that I knew nothing about caring for a baby. I had never had little brothers or sisters or cousins close by. Also, my mother-in-law and I had a sweet relationship. I was dying to introduce her to her first grandchild.

After some hours I woke up and a nurse taught me how to nurse my baby; it worked. The baby was clearly a genius. Soon I got up and held him. I walked around the clinic with him. Another nurse helped me bathe and change him.

Arturo cried, he nursed again, and I asked if someone could bring me a meal. I was starting to get fidgety—where were Manolo and his mother? I showered, I dressed, I nursed the baby, I changed him, I got hungry again. Where were they? Another mother came in to deliver, and I had to move my things out into the hall.

What was holding them up?

I thought about Manolo on the island—what could he be doing there? And suddenly I knew. He was drinking, celebrating with his friends, while we waited. I hugged Arturo close; I didn't tell him what his father was up to.

When at last Manolo got to the clinic, I think I was too relieved to complain.

 # *35 The Island Comes to Cancún in Motorboats*

The young men from the island came to Cancún in two motorboats, five in one twenty-four-foot open boat, six in the other. It was a long way on the choppy sea that windy October day.

When there is *bonanza*, the calm that often accompanies a full moon, the sea is glassy. Then *lanchas* zoom over the water. They motor eastward to round Cabo Catoche and pass to leeward of Isla Contoy. Farther south, the *lancheros*, the boatmen, might wave to some cousins setting out from Isla Mujeres. They continue south, tying up at a hotel marina in Cancún after two and a half hours or so.

But on a rough sea, with winds from a northerly storm kicking up whitecaps, the trip can take four hours. It can take five hours. It takes the time it takes, they say, *lleva el tiempo que lleva.*

So the young men from the island filed into the house with their hair standing in peaks like waves, laughing and smelling of salt. My husband's cousins, Beto and Fito. El Changololo, el Mediocubano. They gave us briny hugs and congratulations. The Galván twins, sun-bleached hair plastered to their foreheads. They left their flip-flops at the door and crowded into our main room on broad bare feet. What a surprise, to see one after another entering the little upstairs apartment.

Outside the door, the wind they call *el norte* howled. Maromas took a seat at the table, and so did Metzo-Metz. El Raya and el Gabo hunkered down against a wall. A few of them pulled soggy tee shirts over their heads. Their muscular chests and brown shoulders filled the kitchen as they replaced wet shirts with dry ones they took from el Pitufo's faded backpack.

Manolo started water boiling for coffee. El Raya removed from a sack the fish that they had caught on the way, a sizable pink hogfish with brilliant red eyes. "Just the ticket for a nursing mama," he smiled at me, setting it into the sink.

"Do you want to see the *chavalo*?" Manolo asked them. That was what they had come for, I now understood. In our little bedroom, our three-day-old son Arturo was asleep in his *moisés*, his wicker cradle with its half-hood like a band shell over his head.

"Band shell" described the top of the cradle perfectly, because our tiny baby was the show. He was the attraction that had lured all these young men on such a rugged journey. Lying on his tummy the way Mexican doctors directed parents to position their babies back then, he was asleep.

"*¡Está embrocado!*" the young men complained to each other in whispered indignation, "He's lying face down!"

They couldn't see his face. They could see his shiny dark hair and a little of the smooth olive skin of his neck. The rest of him was only a long lump under the soft red-and-yellow blanket his godmother had crocheted.

Nobody wanted to wake the baby. But the young fishermen stared at his back, willing him with their eyes to roll over. After an edgy silence, Manolo lifted the bottom of the blanket to show them the baby's little tucked-up legs.

"Look at his feet!" el Changololo exclaimed in a stage whisper. "They look like snorkeling fins!"

Our baby's feet were miniatures of Manolo's, long and very broad at the toes. They were like the feet of all of the young men from the island. Like all the feet in the room, except mine.

"He has fins, like his papá! " declared Metzo-Metz.

"Like his grandpa!" they all agreed happily.

Back in the main room they drank their coffee with plenty of sweet condensed milk, jabbering and making jibes at one another. This baby was the first for their set—everyone asserted that someone else already had the next one on the way.

We offered to put them up for the night, on hammocks and sofa and floor, but no, they went back out into the gray northerly afternoon, into the lanchas and the roaring ocean, back to the island. They had seen what they came to see: feet like fins.

36   *Socorro Interviews for the Job*

On the day Arturo was born, when Manolo showed up at the clinic to take me home, he had already left his mother, a younger sister and two younger brothers at our apartment above the school.

I was so glad to see everyone, I didn't care at all how many were going to stay with us. After all, Manolo's mother had come to help me care for the baby, and I was sure I would need that help. She had expertise, as the mother of seven—in fact, like many of the local mothers, she looked as if she were expecting another. Anyway, she and I had always enjoyed each other's company, and I loved Manolo's little sister and brothers, too.

My only disagreement with my mother-in-law was this: I intended to use disposable diapers for the baby, while Doña Rosalba thought I should wash cloth diapers.

"I'm not going to do that," I protested. Doña Rosalba narrowed her black eyes and asked Manolo, "If she didn't want to wash diapers, why did she have a baby?"

I laughed when I heard that, and I never heard it again.

For one month our three generations played together. I ate Doña Rosalba's delicious dishes and learned about caring for a baby. Carmen came to visit with her baby boy, born the day after Arturo. Former Xicalango teachers, new teachers, the International Women and dozens of students present and past came to marvel at Arturito and bring him little shirts, crocheted caps or linen gloves so he wouldn't scratch his tiny face. At last, though, it was time for Doña Rosalba's crew to leave—the young aunt and uncles had to get back to school, and Don Leandro needed his wife at home.

So I put an advertisement in *NoVerdades* just as I did when we were looking for a teacher. The real name of our daily paper was *Novedades de Quintana Roo,* News of Quintana Roo, but we liked calling it *NoVerdades*, No Truths. Anyway, this time I requested a full-time nursemaid and housekeeper. Friends told me the going rate, and I doubled that figure, hoping to get the best help around. By U.S. standards it was still a small salary for a big job.

The day the ad appeared I got five calls on our brand-new phone. The first caller had a charming voice, and she asked the name of the baby. It pleased me that she wanted to get to know him already. We made a date to meet the next day. Her interview was the first of nearly twenty.

Just before the appointed hour, Socorro knocked on the door of our apartment above the school and stepped over the threshold, her *huipil* dress sparkling and the white eyelet *justán* slip peeking out just so at the hem.

In no time Arturito was on Socorro's lap. She chatted with us in Spanish and with Arturo in Mayan as he lay looking up at her. Need I mention that Manolo and I were gaga over our little Arturo, the smartest and most handsome one-month-old on earth? Well, so was Socorro, evident in how wide she opened her eyes to look at him, and the thousand fine creases at the corners of her lips as she cooed in Mayan, *"Ba'ax ka wa'lik, chan xipal?"* How are you doing, little boy?"

Asking for references, I got the story of her life, related briefly and with a smile. Socorro grew up in Tibolón, a small town not far from Mérida, but a ten-mile walk from the nearest bus route. After she married and had a baby, she became very ill, and did not recover for more than a year. Her mother took care of her and the baby, but eventually Socorro's young husband told her he couldn't handle living with an invalid for so long. He left town and never returned. When at last she was well, it was her turn to leave town, to earn an income to support her parents while they raised her child. In her twenties, Socorro found work as a nanny in Mexico City. There she cared for the family of a doctor. She learned

Spanish, Mexican-style cooking, and how to deal with a climate
much colder than that of the Yucatán.

Ten years with one family, then eleven years with a family in
San Cristóbal, Chiapas. Her daughter was grown by then and
married, and Socorro returned to the Yucatán peninsula, where she
worked for la Señora Isabel de Político in Cancún for a time.

"Señora Isabel?" I exclaimed, "She's my friend!" It was a white
lie. Señora Isabel was the one who had left me in the lurch six years
earlier, after proposing that we start a school together. So the tiny
woman in front of me was the maid Isabel had called "Maria," like
all her other Marias, the one who had brought milk for my coffee.
What a nice coincidence. Although I had other interviews set up, I
was already leaning toward this charming Socorro.

"Let me show you the kitchen," I said to her. With little
Arturo in my arms, I walked down the steps with Manolo and
Socorro. Against the garden wall at the bottom of the staircase
grew a sizable dark-green shrub with many-fingered leaves, pointed
like those of a maple tree. I didn't know how the bush got there; I
only knew not to touch it, because people said it stung.

But Socorro looked at it like a long-lost friend.

"La chaya, Doña Déborah, is the most healthful plant in the
region," she confided. "Have you ever tasted *huevos con chaya,* or
brazo de reina, or a *licuado de chaya with limon?* Especially now that you
are nursing Arturito, chaya is full of iron and vitamins for you."
She ducked into our plain little kitchen and came out with two
transparent plastic bags.

Then Socorro spoke in Mayan directly to the chaya plant, a
soft "shshsh x-cushushush."

"I said to it," she explained, *"comadrita,* dear little godmother,
please lend me some of your leaves so that I can feed my family."
Putting a plastic bag over each hand, Socorro plucked six or eight
big leaves from the ends of the branches.

In the kitchen she stretched high to take the frying pan down
off a hook. A bottle of cooking oil was on the counter along with a
head of garlic. She minced some with deft hands, sautéed it quickly,
then added the chaya leaves to the pan straight from the bag.

"Once you cook the chaya a minute," Socorro said, "the spines disappear."

I handed her the tortillas she requested and some strands of Oaxaca cheese from the refrigerator. In no time Socorro was serving me and Manolo a dish of delicious and magically nutritious *quesadillas de chaya.*

Yes, we interviewed other candidates for the job. But Socorro knew how to talk to adults, babies, and even plants—she had to be the one.

By the way, if you are ever in deep water, or in trouble of any kind, yell, *¡Socorro!* It means "Help!"

37 *Dulce María Speaks Sweetly*

The entire beginner's class leaned forward to hear Dulce María's sweet voice and see her plump, dark lips dance as she struggled to pronounce a sentence in English. She had joined the group late, after the term had begun; her presence brought new excitement to the class.

With Dulce there, the men stayed on their toes. I noticed some women trying to imitate her musical way of speaking, too. We were up to the unit in which the class questions a volunteer about the person standing in the front of the room. "How old is Dulce María?" one student asked.

"She's nineteen."

"Where is she from?

"She comes from Acapulco, Las Cruces," the volunteer told us.

"Is her hair short?"

"No, it's long." And wavy and blue-black, like Superman's.

"And her eyes?" "Black too." And large. Her skin was the color of caramel candy. She was short and, Roberto, the volunteer, asked me, "How do you say, *como mango*?"

"Curvy." I drew an hourglass in the air. What a commotion that raised!

A previous secretary had just left to have her baby. One of the teachers had suggested we find some muscular thug to charge the students their tuition, but Dulce María's sweet sexiness seemed like a better idea to me. She was overjoyed with the job offer.

With Dulce as secretary, the reception area was better organized than before, and more popular. Many students paid their tuition in full at the beginning of the course, which meant more consistent attendance and a lower dropout rate. More students were completing three or four courses without a break, and many became fluent in less than a year.

I was often amazed at the progress our students made—fluency in less that a year? I hadn't seen anything like that in New York. How was this happening?

Well, I realized, aside from their ninety-minute daily classes, most of the students worked at jobs where they used their new English the rest of the day. The more outgoing they were in English, the more money they earned as handicraft salespeople, as waiters or taxi drivers, and the more friends they made. The classmates of one high school boy called him *"El Bilingüe."* In general, whatever their social group, our students got respect.

Also, Xicalango students were a self-selected group. They had chosen to come to the school themselves, and they were paying the tuition out of their salaries.

I loved the mix of students, boys and girls, men and women. In English we have no designated "polite" forms of address. Nevertheless, listening to the young students speaking to their elders, you could hear that polite form even though our language is lacking the special words for it.

The majority of the students were *yucateco*s, from all over the peninsula. Unless they hailed from Mérida, it was safe to assume that Mayan was their first language and that they had learned Spanish in school. In class after class it became clear to me that it is easier to learn a third language than a second.

It seemed to me that people from central Mexico had the upper hand in Cancún. Usually they had more education than the *yucateco*s. The majority of business owners and managers were from central Mexico; the workers on the lowest rung were usually locals. But the Mayan speakers were learning English as a Third Language. I felt proud of them when soft-spoken locals raised their hands and volunteered to "be teacher."

Fortunately, the rivalry between the *huaches* (people from the center of the republic) and the *mayitas* that existed elsewhere rarely came into play in our classrooms. Students sat wherever they found an empty seat and partnered with whoever sat beside them. Pair practice meant that students learned through creative collaboration with their partners. Often partners bonded and made a point of sitting together for months.

Most of the time when a conflict flared, it was over registration. Classes filled up quickly. Then a student due to begin Level 2 or 3 would come to register on the first day of class, only to find his space had been filled. Dulce María would use her "living doll" voice to diffuse bad feeling; then she would work fast to find alternatives.

Another issue was the teacher with the chronic case of *"lunitis,"* a condition that often caused him to miss Monday morning classes. Dulce María would find someone to cover for him, or would step in herself, with a lesson she had just learned in the class she was taking. Someone else underqualified to teach would have elicited complaints—Dulce won praise. "We want Dulce!" students would chant.

One difficulty presented itself when parents came late to pick up their precious adolescent daughters. The girls could sit in the waiting area in front of the school, but occasionally a cluster of fourteen-year-olds would wander off, and then Dulce María would catch hell from the late-arriving mothers. What to do? She got the girls on her side with a nail file and couple of bottles of nail polish; Dulce María suggested the girls give each other manicures while they waited. No more angry *mamás.*

Dulce María was excellent with *mestizos* and with the hoi poloi. She became a star at our *Viernes Sociales,* when all the classes gathered for the last half hour of class for a sing-along. She helped me choose the songs, and I soon realized she had a finger on what people were dying to sing. Dancing around the room, she led seventy-five or eighty of us while we belted out "Girls Just Want to Have Fun."

After some time, Dulce María confided in me about her difficult childhood and youth. In spite of her hardships, the young woman had learned the tact and thoughtfulness that won her so many friends and admirers.

Every year I'd gathered my friends for Thanksgiving dinner, but Dulce Maria's first year some teachers suggested we invite all the students. We decided it would be nice if Dulce María would make the announcement. She started by telling the students about the custom of Thanksgiving.

"Thanksgiving," Dulce María said to one class in her sweetest voice, "is a holiday we gringos always…" That's as far as she got, before the whole crowd of students shouted her down!

38 Inés Saves the Day

Two weeks after the class had begun, the newest student in my Book 2 group was game—Inés was responding in English to every personal question the other students could throw at her. She was from Texcoco, near Mexico City. She worked at Hotel Camino Real, where she was the head of the human resources department. She had six sisters and brothers, and about a thousand nieces and nephews. She had no children, and no, she wasn't married. She spoke French. Also she liked to eat French (French bread, that is, the typical facetious answer to "Do you speak French?") She had a master's degree in industrial psychology and another in anthropology. Once more, she wasn't married. Did she have a boyfriend? "Why only one?" Inés shot back.

I couldn't think of one other woman like her among all the students I had met at the school. There had been a few women doctors and dentists, but married. Several women students were lawyers and executives, but they were very full of themselves. Inés, on the other hand, had a sense of humor.

She was beautiful in a very Mexican way. Somehow *she* managed to avoid telling us her age, but she was no "twenty-something." Her light cotton blouse and gathered skirt of pure white accentuated her coppery complexion, and she was wearing a kind of shoes I had never seen before, low-heeled transparent plastic Mary Janes—within weeks, they were the hot new style. In fact, Inés seemed to be just *my* style. I invited her back to the house after school one chilly night, and our friendship began over Socorro's *caldo de pollo*.

Inés adored baby Arturito. Each time she saw him they would start playing Mexican patty-cake games together. She invited the two of us to have lunch at a beachside Camino Real restaurant, where the barman mixed for my son a delicious virgin piña colada, and served it to him in his sippy cup. Another evening it was Inés's turn to be night manager for the hotel. Arturo stayed with Manolo while Inés and I, dressed to the nines, enjoyed a superb dinner, then danced at the disco overlooking the water, compliments of the Camino Real family of hotels. We were hotel royalty for a night.

At Escuela Xicalango, Inés finished Books 2, 3 and 4. An American woman named Barbara, a birder *extraordinaire* and one of the founders of Sian Ka'an World Heritage Biosphere, asked me to find her a Spanish teacher, and I recommended Inés. Barbara thanked me repeatedly for sending her the perfect teacher.

Then Renée, my beloved French "sister-out-law," came to my house, fleeing the island and the alcoholism of Manolo's older brother; she needed a place to stay, quick. I described the situation to Inés, and she invited Renée to share the house Camino Real had assigned her. Inés and Renée soon became close.

But a few months later, Camino Real decided Inés was needed at the Hotel del Prado in Mexico City, where she had worked earlier. Sadly she gave me her plants and other pretty things she had accumulated in Cancún. Back she went to Mexico City, to live in her Zona Rosa apartment, while Renée found herself another place.

I stayed at Inés' apartment with her for a few days the following year, 1984. We were joined by my New York friends Sylvia and her daughter Suzie. We made forays to Xochimilco, to the *Ballet Folklórico*, and to Popocatepetl, returning to sleep at our cozy base, Inés' place.

Inés and I stayed in touch by mail and phone, maintaining our friendship with frequent contact. So on the morning of September 19th, 1985, when the radio reported a disastrous earthquake in Mexico City, my first impulse was to call Inés on the phone. I knew it wouldn't work. The radio reported that the worst damage was downtown, near her neighborhood. Surely the phones would be out of order, but I called anyway. Inés answered. Shaken, literally.

"The building across the street collapsed in front of my eyes," she told me. I don't know how many people are inside. I can't even see the building now, there's so much dust in the air." As we talked, the air cleared a bit. *"Ay, dios,"* she sighed, "The building looks like a sandwich somebody sat on."

Inés's family was fine, she told me when she called back in the evening, but the hotel where she worked was a wreck. It was the beautiful old Hotel del Prado, with the mural "Dream of a Sunday Afternoon in the Alameda" by Diego Rivera in the lobby. There was no telling when she would work again.

Meanwhile, Escuela Xicalango was an emotional disaster area, with all the *capitalinos* frantic to know about their families. Newspapers were printing the names of the dead; my students wanted to know if their families were alive. No one else I spoke with had established phone communication with loved ones. I felt so lucky to know that my Inés was okay. Fatality rates were rising fast.

"I don't know what to do with myself," Inés said to me on the phone the next day. She had never gone a day without working in her adult life. And it was so sad all around her. I told her about the Xicalango students who couldn't bear to come to school because they couldn't think about anything but their families.

"You know," she said slowly, "I could go and look for those families. I don't have anything *else* to do."

So that evening, three nights after the quake, the teachers notified the students that we were starting a list of addresses of Mexico City families of Xicalango students. By then some people had heard news, but others had no idea how their parents had fared. TV news featured horrendous scenes, and people were still being extricated from the ruins of the General Hospital and the apartment buildings at Tlatelolco. It was hot in the city, the water supply was low, and aftershocks reverberated through panicky neighborhoods. This was the only news.

One student started the list with: "Marina and Alfonso Gutiérrez León, Avenida Aranda #510-A (next to the tailor shop, inside the second wooden door), Colonia Salto del Agua, no telephone." Another printed carefully, "Familia Juarez Baeza, Avenida Independéncia esquina con Dolóres, Edificio Venezuela, interiór #9." Some drew little maps. One added to the address that it was necessary to knock very hard, because the grandmother couldn't hear well. Eleven students wrote addresses for Inés to look for.

Every night after class I would call Inés, and give her several more names and addresses. And every night Inés gave me good news: the people she had sought out were alive and well. It was rough going, she told me. Some bus lines were running, other routes were interrupted by broken pavement or buildings fallen in their paths. *Peseros*, cooperative vans, were the most reliable means of transportation, because they could adjust their routes to suit the crisis. But sometimes she had to walk and wait, walk and wait, then wait some more.

Still, Inés had nothing but success. Success in finding the families, success in finding all alive. None of their buildings had fallen down. Maybe their neighbors' buildings, but not theirs. None were injured, none were starving. All were immensely relieved to have a means to communicate with their sons and daughters, their brothers and sisters and lovers. Some were packing their bags, planning to take the first bus out to Cancún!

It was a tough job Inés was doing, but a vital one. Inés was my dear friend, and her phone line was a lifeline for Xicalango.

39 Running with a Mexican Hero

I was running on the beach with Renée, my "sister-in-law" from France, when a young lawyer I knew ran up alongside us. I introduced them and he gave us kisses on both cheeks, Parisian style. I knew he spoke several languages and I loved the idea of the three of us conversing in French as we ran. He slowed his gait to trot apace with us.

J.L. was tall, with a runner's slim physique. I had heard that he ran ten kilometers daily, and I always saw him at marathons; I'd be running a 5k, while he'd go the full distance. He was dark-skinned with luminous black eyes and a rogue's smile. I had not seen him since reading in the paper that Interpol had come to Cancún to arrest him for stealing a valuable Mexican artifact in Paris. Then I read that the Mexican government had lodged a formal protest against Interpol, insisting that charges be dropped. I was dying to hear about this escapade from the horse's mouth. Had he planned it this way?

"Mais non!" J.L. asserted, "I never planned it at all. It was just that the librarian at the French National Archives was such a *con!*"

I looked to see if Renée was offended, but she was laughing and nodding as if she had had similar experiences with the same librarian.

Little waves lapped at my feet. I was running on the edge of the water, J.L. on my right and Renée on his right. She and I glanced at each other across his smooth brown chest—he was that much taller than either of us.

Renée was more than a friend—she was my *ex-cuñada*, ex-"sister-in-law." And maybe not so "ex." This requires explanation.

Among Mexicans I knew, as soon as a girl makes eyes at a guy, people start making in-law jokes. As far as the jokers are concerned, once a spark is lit between two people, both extended families become instant in-laws.

Renée had lived with Manolo's older brother on the island for most of two years. So I *did* think of her as a sister-in-law. I admired the way she fit into the family, and that she had learned so much island culture. But right now Renée was in Cancún fleeing my brother-in-law. Drinking was the main problem. And drunk, my brother-in-law became abusive, as I had seen. Would he come to Cancún to win Renée back again? Would she go? *¿Quién sabe?* Who knows?

Meanwhile J.L. continued his story. *"Mon dieu!"* he exclaimed, "I went to the Archives to do some research. I was on my way back to Mexico from Egypt, with a few days to spend in Paris. I lead tours groups to Egypt," he explained to Renée, "to demonstrate the commonalities in the Mayan, Aztec and Egyptian pyramids. Have you seen any of my articles about the energy fields in the pyramids? I had one in *El Diario de Yucatán* last month. Anyway, that's why I went to the archives, to study a codex and other ancient texts about the pyramids."

J.L. was a civil lawyer, but a mystic too, with many interests. Many interests, a great deal of knowledge, and a lot of attitude.

"At the archives I requested permission to see two other materials and the Tonalamatl Aubin, there in a reading room. That librarian-*con* questioned me as if I didn't know that I was requesting one of the few remaining pre-Columbian codices in the world. Hmmfff. There's one in Madrid, one in Dresden, one in Mexico City, and the Paris one. *La perra* demanded to hold every document I own. Here I am, a Mexican *juris doctor*, following all the procedures the French government requires, because I want to study a piece of *Mexican* history that was stolen from the Mexican people! And she was acting as if *I* was some jerk, and the codex was her personal property!"

"So I didn't get mad—I just took it! When I returned the other materials I had borrowed to the desk, I 'neglected' to return the

Codex. I had it under the *sarape* I was wearing. She was so busy acting superior that she didn't notice it was missing. That was all."

Renée and I looked in astonishment from J.L.'s grin, to each other, to the turquoise water, and back to him again.

"*Et puis?* Then what happened?" Renée asked. She had had amazing exploits in Mexico, and so had I, but we felt like *ángeles inocentes* next to J.L.

"I brought the Codex back to my apartment here in Cancún. I was studying it. I drew the first four panels and copied the glyphs. I was planning to copy and decipher as much of it as I could. That's when I got word that Interpol was after me. The same day I took the Codex to an archeologist I know at the INAH, the National Institute of Archeology and History. I had been planning to give it to them anyway."

At this point J.L. looked out over the water. I could see Renée was impressed, and maybe attracted, too. In fact, we were both attracted to this intellectual Robin Hood. But I was married, and my husband was home with our baby while I was here running on the beach. *C'est la vie.*

Now we had arrived at the part of the story I had read about in the newspaper. "Local Lawyer Donates Priceless Codex to INAH. Federal Government Lauds Repatriation of Ancient Text To The People of Mexico." Something like that.

Renée and I echoed the sentiments expressed by the newspaper to him. He was a hero. She patted him on the back, while I shook his hand. "*Incroiable!*" we said, "*Felicitacions!*"

"And what's next?" I asked. We were back where Renée and I had begun our run. J.L. was running in place, about to continue.

J.L. looked back at me, white teeth gleaming between his dark lips, eyes alight. There was no one around us. Just before he sped off, in a stage whisper he confided, "Dresden…"

40 *Odalys and the Slammers*

Manolo and I often spent weekends on the boat, taking
tourists to Isla Mujeres during the day, hanging out at the pier long
evenings, watching the sky and water turn pastel colors, drinking
Bohemias or Leon Negra. We liked to swim close to the boat and
bathe Arturo in the warm water. He was no more than two,
walking about carefully on the uneven pier, holding on to the
railings of the sailboat and chattering up at us, big smiles on his
little face.

One late afternoon a surprise visitor came aboard, the brash
and beautiful Odalys. I had met her in my first weeks in Cancún.
After breaking up with her husband she had left for the even newer
resort of Zihuatenejo, and had just returned to Cancún. She was
bubbling about life Zihua. In fact, she had brought with her a
bubbly sample of it: slammers. She had a couple of shot glasses, a
bottle of 7-Up and another of tequila. Slammers were the new
sensation on the Pacific coast, she said. They hadn't yet reached
the bars and parties of Cancún, and Manolo and I had never heard
of them.

"You just fold a dishtowel and put it on the table in front of
you." The boat rocked slightly as Odalys demonstrated, folding the
yellow towel with long brown fingers. "Then you pour the tequila
halfway to the top of a shot glass. You top that off with the 7-Up,
cover the glass with your fingers, and WHAM! You slam it down
onto the dishtowel. That slam mixes it up fast, and you have to
chug it down in one swallow." Odalys demonstrated.

"This way," Odalys laughed, her tawny eyes wide, "the tequila
goes straight to your brain!" Well, sure, we'd try one. The slamming

and the way it bubbled up made it seem like a magic trick. Maybe we'd have another, each of us. They went down easily. That Odalys was so funny! Perhaps Manolo made me a third one...

And then Arturo woke me up. He had scooted his little body up onto the bunk with me, and he was talking his little talk. *"Mamita, quero chocomilk,"* he said. Manolo was asleep where he sat, his back against the galley cabinet. Odalys was laid flat on the other bunk. Arturo had been the only one awake on the rocking sailboat, moored to the dock. Two-year-old Arturo.

I brought Arturo his chocomilk, and stroked his downy brown arms and back with trembling fingers as he drank it. Never again, I promised myself. Never again.

 *41* *We Had It All*

We had it all. We had the graceful Providencia, docked at Hotel Bojorquez. At last we had all the necessary permissions, licenses and authorizations from the Secretary of the Navy, the Port Captain, the seaman's union, the Municipal Government, state government and federal government for the boat to take tourists out on excursions. Manolo was spending most days at the pier, working on the boat, talking up the trip or taking tourists out fishing or to Isla Mujeres.

We had our new home. Years earlier, after a year or so of renting the house on Avenue Nader, I had bought it from the previous owner. Later I bought the adjoining property behind it. When Manolo first came to live with me, we occupied the two-room apartment above the school, and cooked in the school's little kitchen. A few months after Arturo was born, we began building our new place in the back of the yard, replacing a *palapa* that had housed a classroom.

About a year later we moved into our fanciful new residence. I had found a book of colonial-style houses, and had asked an architect to draw up plans incorporating features Manolo and I liked from the houses in the book. I pointed out a picture of a wood-framed quatrofoil window to our skilled young contractor, and he and his team built it, along with everything else we asked for.

The terrace that ran along the front of the house was screened in, with a terracotta tile roof shading it. Hand-painted tiles called *azulejos* that I had bought in Guanajuanto years earlier enlivened the staircase, the window frames and the floor. The wall behind the terrace was composed of accordion-style glass-and-wooden doors that we could leave wide open. At the rear of the house, behind the living room, there were sliding doors of the same materials, so breezes could keep the whole house cool during the hot seasons, without letting in mosquitoes.

The exterior was stucco, sponge-painted a charming pink color characteristic of colonial houses. Set among dark-green lime trees and bright green banana trees, it looked like a house in a fairytale.

We had the time and the money—steady income from the school, and additional income from the boat, so we were able to build just what we wanted. I said we needed three full baths, a shower in each one, so that when we returned from the beach with a dozen islanders or other guests, everyone could bathe without too long a wait. We painted the watertank on the roof black; with Cancún's year-round sun, we rarely needed to use the water heater.

Manolo suggested we decorate the downstairs bathroom with our collection of seashells. The tile in that room was known as *piedra Ticul,* a peach-colored Yucatán travertine. The masons left bare diamond-shaped spaces and fresh plaster for us to use, and Manolo and I spent a wonderful evening arranging olive shells and lion's paws, delicate jingle shells and tough *tomburros* on the fresh plaster. We were overjoyed with the results.

We had Arturo, a healthy, happy and handsome child, the son Manolo and I had both longed for. With Socorro to help me with Arturo, I was able to go back to work a few months after Arturo was born. I could even come home between classes to nurse him during his first year.

But one night while Arturo was still an infant, I sat up in bed, realizing that a bottle had come between my husband and me. It wasn't a baby bottle.

How had I failed to notice this nasty thing any sooner? Was it because, until I became pregnant, that bottle had been community property?

Now that Manolo was captain of the Providencia, he had his own bar on board. He no longer had a supervisor, as he had had with the Fishing Department. He was the registered owner of the beautiful sloop, the only wooden-hulled sailing vessel, the only sailing charter boat in Cancún. And there was no one on board to criticize anything he did.

When Manolo had a trip booked, he needed to use my car to buy sodas and beer, ice, bait, and fuel for the motor. In the evening he would drive home, and proudly flip before my eyes the three-hundred-dollar wad he had earned that day. Arturo and I loved the look in his eyes; we loved to hear what the tourists said about the trip, how they reacted when they caught a fish, what they thought about the boat and the captain.

But by the time we moved into the new house, Manolo was coming home later and later. Sometimes he arrived in a state that we called *"ligeramente tomado,"* or *"tomado;"* other times his state could only be called *"borracho."* Then he was a different person, not the affectionate, gentle person I knew. Drunk, he was always angry, and his drunken strength was frightening to me. He would rant on and on, using some of the same phrases I had heard from his drunkard older brother: fury about the *"sistema,"* fury about everything.

I made him promise he wouldn't drive the car when he'd been drinking. Then I made him promise again. I said he should take a taxi when he'd been drinking, and pick up the car the next day. Then he smashed in the front of my car and the rear bumper of another; I wound up paying to fix both. After the long argument that ensued, I insisted that I'd drive him to the pier with the supplies in the mornings.

My friend Moses, his wife Dalia and their young son came from Israel to visit us just after Arturo turned two. We visited the island, and raven-haired Dalia bustled about, helping with all the preparations for *Día de los Muertos.* She adored the food, the good humor of Don Leandro and Doña Rosalba, how clean and sanitary the indoor-outdoor kitchen was. We took an excursion on the Providencia to Isla Contoy and slept in its harbor. Miles from the coast, under all those brilliant stars, there was nobody but us.

In spite of the celebrations and excursions, though, it was clear to Dalia how difficult the relationship between Manolo and me was becoming. He was in one of his dry cycles, but our conversations had been strained since that car crash. I was seeing a psychologist, and I told Dalia about it. I told her I couldn't fathom breaking up with Manolo—I didn't know how I could raise Arturo without him.

Arturo liked to walk between Manolo and me, holding our hands and swinging while we sang a song my parents had sung to me. It must be a '30s or '40s pop song: dee DUM, dee DUM, dee diddle-de-DUM de DUM. That phrase repeats, a chorus of dee DUMs follows, and then the music crescendos in DEEDLY DEEDLY DUM. Arturo wanted to be swung all the time, but we got him into the habit of singing the song with us; when we reached the crescendo we'd swing him way up high. Knowing that the flight was coming made the song thrilling for him, beginning to end.

But if Manolo and I separated and Arturo had only one parent's hand to hold, what would happen on the DEEDLY DEEDLY DUM? The thought had me in tears.

And then there was the island. If I broke up with Manolo, would the island be lost to me too? And, I thought, Arturo looked so much like Manolo—how could he grow up right, without the parent who apparently had contributed the sea lion's share of the genes? I couldn't answer any of this for myself. And so the relationship wore on, wearing me to a threadbare rag of myself.

Dalia is a *sabra*, born in Israel to Yemenite parents. Wherever we were, people mistook her for Mexican. Strong physically and strong of character, too, she did not hold her tongue about my difficulties with Manolo.

"You HAVE to tell his mother!" she insisted. "If you two break up, she HAS to know what was going on!" I shook my head. I was so fond of Doña Rosalba. She had given me an entire month of her life after Arturo was born, and so much more. What if telling her should turn her against me? Weeks went by. After Moses and Dalia left, an especially bad period began with Manolo, and I realized I had no choice.

In fact, Doña Rosalba was nodding in agreement as soon as I began describing our current situation. Manolo's problem drinking had started long before he ever left the island, she admitted. But it was not unusual behavior there. Locals liked to brag that their island had the highest beer consumption per capita in the republic. Since there were no paved roads and no cars to drive, a good drunk typically resulted in nothing worse than a hangover.

"When he comes home *tomado*," Doña Rosalba said to me, "just give him something to eat and let him go to sleep. Why don't you try that?"

A few days or weeks later Manolo came in roaring. Someone had cheated him on the boat, somebody had misused him and he was going to holler at me about it, at midnight, and wake up the baby. I went downstairs to the kitchen and heated up the pork chops in tomato sauce and beans and tortillas from dinner.

Manolo had not sat down at the table, and I was talking to him as I handed him the plate, reprimanding him, I'm sure. I don't remember what he said, but I remember the pork chop slapping my cheek, the tomato sauce in my eye. I heard the plate smash on the tile floor.

Maybe this was the time I went to the church and talked to the padre about our problem. Maybe this time Manolo went there with me, and agreed again to go to AA. Or maybe this was the time he went to the marriage counselor with me. Maybe he stayed dry for a month.

Then one morning I lent Manolo the car to pick up some new life vests and take them to the pier. That night he never came back home. The next day his friend Rubén came to tell me Manolo was in jail. He had run over the legs of some poor man who was sitting on a curb waiting for a bus, and both the man's legs were broken.

"That is it!" I sobbed. "Jail is the right place for him," I cried to Rubén, "I am *not* going to get him out. This is the end!"

Three days later Rubén came back, pleading with me to get Manolo out of jail. "He is still wearing nothing but the bathing suit they arrested him in!" Rubén wailed. "He's filthy, he's starving—they treat the prisoners like dogs!"

I couldn't stand it. Rubén walked me to the *Ministerio* and there I signed a document saying that I would be responsible for him. I brought him home on some condition, some condition he had already promised to and broken many times before.

So we started the last new beginning of our relationship. It was winter now, and the boat wasn't going out much, what with all the *nortes*, northerlies. Manolo had not gone to see the man he had hit, but I insisted he talk to him. Finally he told me he had visited, and that the man accepted him, accepted the accident as God's will.

"Drunken driving is *not* God's will," I said.

I think he stayed dry that time for three months, drinking nonalcoholic beer through Christmas and New Year. He built Arturo a little play structure in the yard, with an old canvas sail for its floor. He built shelves and installed kitchen cabinets; he planted cilantro and watered the lime tree. When I left the classroom I would see Arturo setting off at a toddle around our block, hand-in-hand with Manolo.

The police had revoked Manolo's driver's license, and I forbade him to use my car again. He took the bus or got a ride to the pier. But one night I woke up to him roaring again, with the car keys in his hand and Arturo astride his hip. "It's YOUR *pinche* car," he yelled, "and your school and everything is yours, but this is MY SON!"

He was down the stairs and out to the car before I could catch him. The car screamed away down Avenue Nader into the black night.

In my robe and slippers I ran around the block hoping to hear the car. I threw a jacket on over my nightgown and took a cab to the pier at two in the morning—all was quiet there, except for the crash scenarios in my brain.

In the morning Arturo was sleeping in his little bed, my car keys were on the kitchen table, and I didn't see Manolo again for a week or more.

But this time I got a restraining order. Many police officers had been students, and in fact I knew the chief of police from that day long before when I thought they had offered to "send a *perrito*" to check for fingerprints. The chief promised me that officers would keep an eye on the school and the entrance to my house for as long as I needed it. They were there for a few days, and I knew I could call the police department when necessary. But I also knew they couldn't place an officer on constant vigil at my house. I changed the lock on the gate that led into our front yard.

Socorro would tell me that Manolo came to visit Arturo when he knew I was in class. On more than one occasion he came to the locked gate at night and I wouldn't open it. Sometimes he came sober and repentant, sometimes he came angry, beating on the door. Sometimes I called the police to chase him away.

I changed the locks on the school, too, but Manolo had some secret way of getting in. Late some nights, Socorro stood at my side in the house, looking through a window at the darkened school, and the glow of a cigarette burning inside. In the morning he was gone, and our lives went on without him.

42 Braking for Phantoms

In the 'seventies and 'eighties, if you wanted anything more than the most basic items, you had to go to Mérida. It was a pleasure anyway. The two-lane highway was as straight as a Mayan ponytail. It was punctuated by villages, little gatherings of palm-thatched cottages. Women chatted as they carried orange or pink buckets of corn kernels on their heads toward the mill, or the same buckets filled with masa for tortillas (ground corn dough), back home again.

Many villages had histories for me. One hamlet had a particularly lovely kind of tree shading many of the thatched palapa houses. It must be a fast-growing tree, I felt sure, because they were in full leaf all through the town, but I remembered seeing only one such tree the year before.

A showy tree it was, with large, heart-shaped leaves. Each leaf was a pale creamy yellow, with a central vein and ten or twelve lateral veins of rich dark green. Even from a distance you could see that the leaves were striped, unlike any other tree I knew.

I decided to pull over near a house graced with two of these trees. They grew symmetrically, with a broad, rounded crown above a silky trunk. I wanted to ask the homeowner what kind of tree it was, and sure enough, a smiling man emerged from his cottage as my car neared the stone wall surrounding his property.

"Buenas tardes," I began, "Would you mind telling me what kind of tree that is?"

"Oh, you like it? " he replied brightly. "Wait," he said, indicating with an inch of space between his thumb and forefinger the length of time that he would need. He returned quicker than it takes to write about it, carrying a yellow bucket with some water in the bottom, a bunch of old newspapers, some of the local Yucatán twine called mecate and a machete. Still smiling, he strode to the larger of the two trees and WHOP! he lopped off a hefty branch. With the fourteen-inch machete he trimmed it swiftly, leaving only the main limb and two or three small twigs attached, with a few curled leaves emerging.

Talking all the time, he wrapped the cut stem in newspapers and tied it with the *mecate*. "My *compadre* brought me a branch of this tree from Tizimín just two years ago," he told me, adding the name of the *compadre*, the *comadre*, the infant he had christened for them, and some comments about what they had eaten at the

christening. Then he thrust the branch into the bucket, which I now realized he was ready to discard, because it had a hole halfway up from the bottom. The *Diario de Yucatán* newspaper absorbed the water, and the cut end of the branch was moist and insulated for a journey.

"Keep it wet," he instructed, holding the bucket out for me. "Plant it in three nights, after the new moon. Not too close to your house. It will fuck up the foundations in a year or two if it's too

close. Be sure to water it well the first few weeks." I stood blinking
and smiling as I took the bucket from him. I had only meant to ask
the tree's name, and here I was carrying home a jewel of a plant,
unknown in Cancún.

In the fierce sunlight in front of the school, the cutting became
a wonderful shade tree. I never did find out its name.

Years later in another town, little Arturo and I were looking for
a bathroom—there were no gas stations along this road for hours,
no restaurants, nothing "public." Next to the plaza was the town's
only two-story building—the police station with its little jail. I
asked help of a man in a blue guayabera shirt and mustard-colored
polyester pants. He told me that the only bathroom in town was
there, in the *"Delegación de Policía."* I pushed the door open and saw
the Police Force—well, maybe he was half of the Police Force. His
back was upright in his swivel chair, but his chin was buried in his
uniformed chest. He was snoring in a deep tenor. In order to relax
in comfort, he had removed his thick belt with its leather holster
and its gun. It was lying on the desk, very close to Arturo and me
as we stole across the tiny office to the bathroom. We certainly
didn't want to bother the officer, and his snoring continued
uninterrupted.

Arturo used the toilet first. He was only three or four at the
time, and he needed a little help. For example, he needed help to
find the toilet paper. It wasn't in the toilet paper dispenser; there
was nothing there, not even a metal cylinder to hold the roll. Then
I noticed that there were torn leaves of paper in the sink, as was
common. Usually it was *Noverdades*, our newspaper. But no, these
small, square leaves of paper were not from the newspaper. They
came from The Official Manual of the Federal Police Force of the
Republic of Mexico. There might have been two hundred sheets of
fine print. Toilet paper aplenty.

Swallowing my laughter, I explained in a whisper to Arturo,
and he joined me in smothered hilarity. Once we got ourselves

under control, we tiptoed out. Wouldn't want to disturb a man doing his job.

But one time on the road back to Cancún, after a Mérida shopping spree, we found ourselves in a situation that was not so amusing. We had left "The White City" late, considering the four-hour drive. About an hour and a half out of town the sun descended and light fled quickly, as it does in the tropics. But it was not only the afternoon light that faded—my headlights were fading too. The dashboard lights dimmed and disappeared, and ahead of me I could barely see the road.

Arturo had fallen asleep in the back seat. His skinny frame fit head to toe between one side and the other of the VW bug. The road was straight and narrow, two lanes all the way from Hacienda Tekax to Cancún. It had slight curves, though, and I could hardly anticipate them. Fortunately, few cars were on the road. One old pick-up flashed his brights at me furiously. We had passed one village before I understood what was happening, and there were still eight or ten kilometers to travel before the next village.

Driving in dimness, I leaned as close to the windshield as I could, braking slightly for phantoms. Dark brush to one side, Yucatán rock walls to the other. Driving in near darkness, then in darkness. I was driving blind, the steering wheel sweaty in my grip. Arturo was silent, but I kept grinding my teeth and sucking my lips into knots.

Then a dim halo appeared on the horizon. It could only be the next little village. The halo brightened, and we were closer. I think I was driving slower than ten kilometers per hour, though I couldn't be sure—the dashboard might as well have been a slab of slate. Gracias a Dios, we were finally approaching a little town.

Those villages didn't have electricity yet. People lit their houses with gas lanterns or candles. Six o'clock on a Sunday night, families would be walking to or from church in the dark, staggering down the road drunk, chattering as they entered the little stores stocked with little more than crackers and condensed milk, illuminated with one Coleman lamp. Was a drunk, or a child, or a mother with child, on the road before me?

The car was rolling at a pedestrian's pace as I slid up beside a little open-air bar. One lantern, five or six men at two folding tables. *Chac pol* is what they were drinking. Corn liquor, harsh as punishment. Perhaps it had been bottled right there in that little bar, and stopped up with a "red head, " the *"chac pol"* for which it was named.

"¿Qué ondas?" they greeted me, what's going on? No one had missed the gravity of the situation. Flashlights were produced, and a blanket appeared to cover Arturo. Two men were under the hood and one under the car in no time. *'Tux ca'bin?'* they asked, Mayan for "Where are you going?" Silence when I answered that I was going to Cancún. It was nearly three hours off. There were no questions about why I was traveling alone with a child on this solitary road. No one asked where my accent came from, or what I would do if I couldn't continue. All their attention was directed toward this odd automotive problem.

Shortly they found the cause: the fan belt that drives the electrical system had somehow stretched. Did I have a spare fan belt? I should have had one, but I didn't. There were two trucks but no cars in the village. No one else would have a fan belt for me. A miracle was required.

How do you tie a knot in a fan belt to shorten it? I had no idea. But they did. They put a short, smooth piece of wood inside the knot to secure it. The knot was similar to the ones they use to tie up a hammock, and those knots better hold while you're making love, or you've got one aching lover.

The knot was tied, the belt was in place, they ran the engine and—bright headlights illuminated a sizable gathering. This was the place to be! We laughed and patted each other on the back. *Dios bo tik,* may God repay you for this, I said all around.

But still, was this jerry-rigging going to be good enough? Would it get me all the way back to Cancún tonight, with my little boy asleep in the back seat? Mayan conversations ensued that I couldn't follow.

Finally a man pushed a slim, smiling preadolescent in front of me. "Take Felipe," he said. "Take my son Felipe along with you in case anything goes wrong. If you should need to leave the car, you can't leave *el tsi'rits,* the little one, alone. Take Felipe. You can drop him at his cousin's house when you get to Cancún."

"Really?" I gasped. "Are you sure?"

"Sure, " the man chuckled, "he gets a little vacation. How much will you charge for the ride?"

Everybody got a good laugh out of that, and then we three headed off to Cancún.

43 Don Irving in Cancún

Eleven times my father visited me in Cancún, grumbling each time. His feet were always swollen upon arrival. "Don't they have any air conditioning in this airport?" he would ask first. Usually his next question was "Aren't they *ever* going to start selling *The New York Times* here?"

In fact, my situation in Cancún did not offer much to keep this intellectual New Yorker busy. He missed his piano. He didn't speak Spanish, and he wasn't an outdoor type. Childhood polio had left Irving with a tricky knee, which made walking on the beach hazardous for him. He loved strolling with me in town, though, especially when people stopped us to ask, *"Maestra,* when does the next course begin?" If they were already Xicalango students, there was a good chance they would give me a hug, and add a respectful smile and a handshake for Don Irving. The women might give him a kiss on the cheek too. Then he would tell me that I should be the mayor of Cancún.

Hungarian and Romanian by heritage, Irving looked Mexican. I have my mother's blue eyes and olive skin that tans well. My dad was swarthier, his heavily lidded eyes nearly black. Our height was about the same: diminutive. Irving was rather rotund, in a way that is typical of both Eastern European and Mexican older men. His wavy hair stayed dark into his seventies, along with his trim beard and mustache. His eyes had a twinkle to them—in fact, people mention his sense of humor almost as often as they recall his hurricane temper. Although he spoke only un *poquito* de español, he loved putting on the dog. He practiced telling time in Spanish, and during visits he trolled the neighborhood, waiting for *mexicanos* to notice his big, shiny watch and ask him the time of day.

The first years I was in Cancún, I had no phone and neither did anyone else I knew. Irving and I communicated only through letters. On one of my visits to New York in the 'eighties, he waved a chunky parcel at me in reproach—"This is *all* you've sent me in all these years! What am I supposed to do, read them over and over?" To me it looked like a nice thick stack, and I was pleased he had kept them so carefully.

Later he calmed down and read an early letter to me proudly. I had written him that I would teach English in the hotels until I could open a school. "There will be all kinds of people in my school, and it will be a social center as well as a school. We'll sing, and make parties and take trips. I'll play tennis in the evenings, and go snorkeling on weekends, and I want to learn all about the Mayans..."

This letter must have been ten years old when he read it to me. "I don't know anyone but you who has accomplished exactly what they set out to do," he told me. Once, at a Hanukkah party at the Queens, New York Jewish Community Center where he was a part-time social worker, he introduced me to his co-workers and clients in a way that gave them pause: "This is my daughter Déborah, from Mexico." The pride he showed in me helped me disregard the grousing that accompanied it.

Early in 1985, when Irving was eighty years old, my brother called from Atlanta to say we would need to put our father into a home—he had dementia, Geoffrey asserted. I knew this couldn't be true—I had received a classic Irving letter just a week earlier. He wrote about some critical characters at the JCC Senior Center: "These old people are never happy!" he complained.

Irving mentioned what the doctor had said about his diabetes treatment on a recent visit. There were allusions to the problem of dividing holiday time between his two girlfriends. As always, he harangued me about the infrequency of my letters and calls.

But my brother insisted there was real trouble, so I arranged subs for my classes and took three-year-old Arturo to his

grandparents' place on the island. They assured me I could leave
him as long as needed. Then I flew into a New York January. I no
longer owned shoes with closed toes. By the time I reached
Jackson Heights my toes were so many little popsicles.

A sickening smell hit me at his door. Irving was at home with a
caregiver my brother had hired, and a horrid infection on his toe, a
common complication of diabetes. He was out of touch, all right,
but when I saw the Johnny Walker Red bottle on the bedside table
next to the medicines, I began to wonder whether it was the
scotch-and-insulin cocktail that was leaving him so loopy.

I took Irving to Long Island General Hospital. Sure enough, a
scotch-free regimen had him back to erudite irritation in less than
two days. He had good reason for it, too. Doctors and nurses
argued loudly in the hallways, blaming each other for lost files.
Nurses woke him to take his meds at 6:00 a.m. The gowns left his
"*kishkas* hanging out in back."

Three weeks later I left Irving at his apartment again. He was
still unable to walk because of the lesion on his foot. Geoffrey
cobbled together a schedule of caregivers, and I flew back to
Cancún.

On the island at his grandparents' house, my boy Arturo
looked brown and well fed. He was happy to be there, and happy
to go home with me and the Mickey Mouse he had asked me for
on the phone. I felt so grateful to the grandparents for taking care
of Arturo, allowing me to care for my father, I had to ask what I
could do for them. Don Leandro thought a moment, shrugged a
shoulder and answered, "Leave him here another month."

A month or two later in Cancún, phone conversations made it
clear my dad's situation was far from stable. The foot was getting
no better. He couldn't walk, and he was stuck in the apartment
with a terrifically expensive merry-go-round of caregivers he didn't
like.

My friend Inés was back in Cancún, and one night soon after
my return, she and I went to see the movie *The Killing Fields,* about
the atrocities in Cambodia. We emerged in anguish.

"What can we do?" we asked each other. We didn't come up with any way we could ease the suffering in Cambodia. But I thought of one human being I could help—my father.

As far as I knew, there were no nursing homes or senior facilities in Cancún. Elderly Mexicans lived on their own or with their children and grandchildren, and that was that. Manolo's grandparents had been revered; the sepia photo of them, seated among their crowd of adult children, sat on an altar adorned with flowers. They were usually referred to as *finada la abuela*, dear departed grandma, and *finadito*. There were several children named after each, and they figured in the conversation daily, though *la abuelita* had been gone a good ten years already.

When Manolo's maternal grandmother had died only the year before, hundreds had gathered for her wake and her funeral. I cooked from her recipes and I had bushes growing from cuttings of her favorite plants.

So what was I going to be—an American daughter, and let my father languish far away? Or *una buena hija*, a good daughter, and bring him home?

Socorro, her mate Juan and I made the downstairs office into a bedroom. We added handrails in the bathroom and rearranged furniture so that a wheelchair could maneuver around the place. Juan would simply have to lift my dad, wheelchair and all, up the three front steps.

It was a questionable plan—what kind of medical care could Irving get in Cancún? But what was he getting in New York? Just a barrage of antibiotics for the infection, and diabetes drugs; he could get both here as well. I don't remember him objecting at all.

Who packed him up and put him on the plane in New York? One of the girlfriends? I don't remember. I do remember the dashing look on his face as a beautiful flight attendant wheeled him ceremoniously down the ramp of the plane for his Mexican adventure.

Don Déboro, some called him. Others called him *Papá*. Socorro and Juan knew him as *El Abuelo*, grandpa. I had many girlfriends; they kissed and pampered him. They brought him soup, they

brought him flan, and on hot days they fanned him. The lovely
Dulce María, the school secretary who had already known Don
Irving through many earlier visits, virtually abandoned her
reception desk to shoot the breeze with him. Finally her English
became fluent. Not long after, she named her newborn son Irving.
There were two teachers from New York at the time, a charming
Nuyorican who rooted for the Knicks on TV with Irving, and a gay
dancer who took him on at chess. Don Irv seemed to win most of
the time.

One hot afternoon Irving asked me if I had any of that
"marinara" for him to try. Once I stopped laughing, I went upstairs
and rolled a joint of some of the best stuff I'd ever had. Before
we'd even finished smoking it, he started complaining that it was
only making his tongue thick, but it wasn't doing anything
else—well, maybe not to him! So there I was, all hypersensitive,
and he, doubly irascible.

He was scrappy, that Irving. Sometimes I came back after class
to find him arguing with little Arturo over whose turn it was to see
their TV program. And he often became exasperated with Socorro,
because she couldn't understand him. But she and Juan were
inexhaustible in their efforts to make *El Abuelo* comfortable.

The best example was the day Irving wanted to do some
shopping on Avenue Tulúm. I heard about this jaunt when I left
my morning classes, so I thought I'd try to meet them.

As I approached Avenue Tulúm, Cancún's eight-lane main
drag, a remarkable sight greeted me. There stood little Socorro in
the crosswalk, thin as a heron in her white huipil dress, straddling
the line between lanes two and three. She held one delicate brown
hand up, palm facing four lanes of oncoming traffic. Juan was
behind her in the median, facing me but gawking at Socorro with
mouth wide open, gripping the handles of Don Irving's wheelchair.
At last the cars in all four southbound lanes came to a complete
stop. Then Juan trundled the triumphant Don Irving across the
street. Irving had that dashing look again.

I wish the story could end there. But after several months it
became clear that Irving needed to be hospitalized again. My friend

Sylvia, the New Yorker who'd goaded me into teaching in Mexico so many years earlier, had a brilliant idea: if we could change Irv's official residence to her address in Manhattan, he would be eligible for Beth Israel Hospital, one of New York's very best. I managed to make the arrangements over the phone, and we took a taxi from Kennedy Airport direct to the hospital. They admitted him quickly. He loved his doctors there—the one he called Cindy Crawford, the other Robert Redford. There was nowhere he could have been better cared for, he said. Nonetheless, he lasted only a month.

But during his eleventh stay in Cancún and my last times with him in New York, Irving and I had resolved our lifetime of difficulties. We had made amends, Mexican style.

44   *Socorro's Hopes and Dreams*

"Doña Déborah, I want to marry a man I read about in *Noverdades.*"

"Oh?"

"He must be a good man, Doña Déborah," Socorro explained excitedly. "He's a religious man. And a religious man who puts an ad for a wife in the paper, I think he must be an older man. About my age."

What was Socorro's age? Who knew? Her brown skin was smooth and tight across her cheekbones, but wrinkled in an infinity of the finest lines beside her eyes and around the corners of her lips when she smiled. Like many *yucateco*s who had not known the benefits of dentistry early on, she looked younger when her mouth was closed.

When she was in her mid-twenties and she spoke Mayan and only a little Spanish, she had once told me, a dentist in Mérida had anesthetized her in order to pull one bad tooth. He gave her an injection and came back in a while, asking, "Is it numb yet? *Está intumido?*"

"*¿Intumido? ¿Intumido?*" Socorro asked herself. Not knowing the meaning of the word, she shook her head, "No." Another injection. "*¿Intumido?*" the dentist asked again. Another shake of the head. The third time she changed her tune: "*¡Sí, intumido!*"

Now she continued explaining the classified ad to me. "The man who wrote the ad is English," she averred, "so he could teach me to speak English. It says he's a pastor, so he must be a good man. And he's looking for a wife. In the newspapers. In *Noverdades.*

I am going to call him." She showed me the number where she had written it in blue ink on the inside of her thin brown forearm.

I knew the fact that he might teach her English was very important. She had only gone to school a few years, but Socorro had made a point of learning some English. After all, for five years now she had been the custodian at Escuela Xicalango, Cancún's finest English school. She was also the cook and bottle washer, and nanny to the son of the director. She liked if I asked her in English to please bring the keys or the saltshaker.

Socorro used to recite a little Hebrew too. She would say, *"Manish ta na ha'lilah hazeh,"* the beginning of the Four Questions from the Passover seder, whenever Jewish friends and relatives appeared. They loved hearing these words in her sweet voice, pride shining from her cheekbones. She had some French, *"Comment ça va?"* and *"Merci beaucoup,"* for Danielle from Quebec and Renée from France. Also *"danke schön"* for Astrid, my German friend. She answered the phone boldly, "Good morning, Escuela Xicalango, can I help you?" She was ready for anything.

"I would like to read this ad in the *Noverdades*, Socorro," I said. "It sounds very odd to me. Would you please show it to me?" Such a skeptic I was. I didn't believe in the power of basil leaves in the ears for earaches, or tiny smooth shells inside the eye to clean out impurities, or others of her many remedies. I had to read it first.

So Socorro left her plastic sling-back shoes in front of the sink and ran to the back garden, where the tortillas were drying in the sun. There she had read the newspaper while breaking the ends off the green beans. Then she had set the page down in the sun. On top of it she had spread the day-old tortillas, to later make *chilaquiles en salsa verde*. The tortillas were dry now, curled in half cylinders, ready to cut up and fry, all light and crispy.

Socorro piled the dried tortillas into a plastic bowl and located the ad on the folded page where she had circled it with a pen. She tucked the front of her *huipil* tunic-dress into the waist of her *justán* half-slip for the hundredth time of the day. Chubby mestizas wore their *huipiles* untucked, like smooth pillowcases falling from neck to knee. But wiry mestizas like Socorro tucked the front into the drawstring waist of the *justán*, their only undergarment. The tuck raises the embroidered hem over the knee, so they can get around faster. She scooted back to the porch with the sheaf of newsprint.

"Here it is, Doña Déborah. Read it."

Among the personals on the classified page was a small ad circled around and around. I read it aloud: *"Pastor inglés* (English Sheepdog) *busca esposa* (seeks a mate). *Teléfono: 54802."*

Who laughed louder, Socorro or me, once she understood? I don't know. But she was the first to tell this joke on herself to friends from near and far.

45 Gavilán and Paloma in Deep Water

Early in the morning before it got hot, I often ran with my dogs, Gavilán and Paloma, on the *ciclopista*, the bike path. Dalmation-Lab mixes, they were reliable runners. About three kilometers from where the *ciclopista* began there was a lagoon, a lovely place where great egrets and snowy egrets, kingfishers and even petal-pink roseate spoonbills would congregate.

The dogs were good swimmers—they had begun swimming with me when we ran near Punta Sam, and they needed no encouragement to plunge into any body of water. I never swam in that little lagoon, but they dove in right away and doggie-paddled from one end to the other.

This time, after the dogs had been in the water a short while, I noticed something, well, actually two things, heading toward them. But it was very strange; the two things, though separated by a few inches, moved at exactly the same speed. They were balls of some sort, protruding from the water and swimming in sync toward my frolicking pets. I stared at the two things until my mind's eye completed the picture—the pair of globes were protuberances over the eyes of an enormous alligator, and he was speeding toward my dear doggies like a silver salesman after a gaggle of spring-breakers!

I began to yell—"Gavilán! Paloma! Gavilán! *¡Salgan! ¡Vengan¡* Get out of there NOW!" Gavilán was always the more obedient of the two. He made it to the shore and started up the slippery bank in an instant. Paloma, more independent, headed for the far shore. She looked back at me defiantly. But an instant later she must have caught a whiff of something; nervously she started scaling the bank.

Gavilán was at my side now, but each time Paloma gained ground, she lost it again on the steep bank of the lagoon. The eyes of the 'gator were like sights on a rifle; as I hunkered down next to Gavilán, I could look between the two eye-humps and see Paloma. This was surely a gigantic animal. Paloma was yelping, Gavilán was barking, and I was screaming "Paloma, ¡córrele!" Then at last the dog found a good foothold. She hauled herself up, slick and shaky, and began running along the perimeter of the lagoon, back toward Gavilán and me. I glanced at the water again in time to see the alligator, its snout nearly touching the shore, open his great jaws in cold-blooded frustration. The teeth were not white—they were metallic gray, like saw blades. The animal's jaws, as long as my arm, yawned open and closed in disappointment.

I hugged my muddy dogs' heads and chided them all the run back home. "Don't EVER go back in that water again, do you hear me? I had no idea! Did you know there were alligators in there?" I asked them. I think they shook their heads. We never saw the beast again. And the dogs never jumped into that dark water again, either.

 *46* *Arturo at Restaurant Xcaret*

My friends from New York were visiting, and along with Carolina the guide, we spent a grand day *turisteando*. We climbed high above the forest canopy to the top of the tallest pyramid at Coba. Later we admired purple gallinules, henlike birds with iridescent plumage, skulking around the edges of the lagoon. In the afternoon we walked single file along a narrow trail to a grotto at Xcaret, a lovely undeveloped spot. Looking into the largest grotto, I noticed nothing that hinted of a miracle. Caro asked us if we saw anything within the cave, and we shook our heads. Then, with magician's timing, she tossed a small stone inside. A brilliant splash arose from hitherto invisible water.

Xcaret was wild jungle fifty-six kilometers south of Cancún. In a palapa beside the road, a small restaurant specialized in game so fresh, you got the feeling the cooks had shot it through an open kitchen window. The menu featured *tzic de venado* (venison salad), tortoise steak in garlic, ribs of wild boar, wild turkey in Yucatán black sauce, and *tik-in-xik* of grouper caught that morning. Black-and-white photographs on the stick walls featured famous pioneers of Quintana Roo displaying lobsters that reached from the men's heads to their knees, and jewfish the size of Volkswagens.

We had a splendid dinner, accompanied by the excellent Bohemia beer and then a good bottle of Spanish red wine. Arturo at three or four years of age chatted with everyone in his fluent Spanglish. The conversation had no pauses.

Except when Arturo needed to use the bathroom. I had eaten at the restaurant a number of times, and knew that the restroom was adjacent to the dining room, immediately outside the door and to the right.

"Go ahead, Arturo, it's right outside that door," I said, pointing.

In no time he was back.

"Hay una araña en la puerta," he informed us dispassionately, a spider in the doorway. His voice was quite thin; I got the impression that it was the eensty weentsy spider.

"Just walk around it," was my suggestion. I took another sip of my wine and tried to wedge myself back into the conversation.

Off he went. And back he came. "The door is open only *un poco*. And the *araña* is right in the middle."

I wanted to say, "Open the door further," but I stood up from the table, and Suzie, Sylvia and Caro followed me to see the spider.

It was a tarantula. A big juicy brown one, hairs prickling alert, filling the narrow space that the door was ajar. I snatched Arturo up, and the four of us took turns hugging and congratulating our wise little man. I thought: this little boy knows when to insist on getting help. I believe this boy is going to make it, whether or not his father is in the picture.

Then I took him by the hand and walked with him to the corner of the clearing that served as a parking lot, where he peed a triumphal arc into the jungle.

47 The Lime Tree

A month or two after my husband and I broke up, I gave him permission to come to the house during the day to play with Arturo. At three years of age, my little boy was so much like his father that people would look at him and say "Manolo must have spit that boy out."

When Manolo arrived, I would often ask him to take Arturo to the park behind our house, or to walk the dogs with him. It didn't matter what I asked him to do; he always did something else. Like water the lime tree. He had planted that little sprig of a tree soon after we moved into this house, and after only one year the tree was fruiting. But now, with him watering it every time I asked him to do anything, it was fruiting like crazy and growing like mad. It was a foot or two taller than I am, and as wide as it was tall. From the kitchen table, you could see the tree's lush, shady branches right through the screens on the terrace.

If Manolo was going to eat with us and I asked him to sit down at the table with Arturo, he would step outside to water the lime tree.

Arturo didn't eat very much. He had gone from being an infant my father described as a "little Mexican truck driver," to being a scrawny toddler, and then a sickly-looking child with skinny arms and legs and a large round belly. He had amoebas about as often as not. The doctor recommended treatment, usually the awful Flagyl; it left Arturo with no appetite. He would finish a fourteen-day treatment with a flat belly and purplish half-moons under his large brown eyes. A month later his little belly would be inflated again.

So there we'd be, Arturo and I, sitting at the table. I'd be waiting for Arturo to pick up a fork while he was waiting for

Manolo to come in from the lime tree. One evening, with Arturo's dinner growing cold in front of him, Manolo came to the door and motioned us to join him.

"You both have to come out and see this."

"See what?" I asked, "I want Arturo to start his dinner."

"You *have* to come and see."

Arturo jumped down from his seat, and I followed. Looking deep into the branches of the lime tree, woven between hard, dark-green leaves, we saw a nest of *yuyas*, hooded orioles. The father bird's wings, face and throat were black and shiny as tar; his belly and the back of his head were the brilliant orange color of California poppies. He was feeding the clutch of chicks, playing fair while five or six hungry beaks cheeped at him. Then the subdued yellowish mother bird poked her way back into the tree with more grub.

Elated with Manolo's discovery, we returned to kitchen table for our dinner. Arturo tipped his little mouth up like a *yuya* chick, and Manolo fed him bits of *carne asada*. We three drank a toast to the *yuya* family, a toast in limeade, from the lime tree.

48   Leaving Cancún

The beach, Cancún's *raison d'etre,* the reason I had fallen in love with it in the first place, was disappearing. Hurricane Wilma and subsequent storms had torn the coastline to pieces, then slapped some bits back on at random. Stormy seas had deposited acres of sand on the Bahia de Mujeres coast, but they had taken those acres from the Caribbean side, my running beach. Huge expanses of jagged black rock, the weathered skeleton of dead reef, were all that was left where smooth sandy beach had been, near Playa Chac Mool and farther south. No one could run over those treacherous patches.

Other areas of the beach had simply fallen off—there was no longer any beach in front of Hotel Krystal, nor was there any a little past the old Hotel Garza Blanca, where I liked to begin my run.

Swimming held new perils, too. The first time I started scratching under my bra, I had no idea where all those welts came from.

The second time, it occurred to me that they were bites, and only on areas that my bathing suit covered. Something in the water had attacked me. It was awful to be covered with bites in places where scratching looked indecent.

The more I thought about it, the more I realized that this condition must be affecting other people too. Then I began noticing men surreptitiously scratching their butts, women rubbing their arms back and forth along the sides of their breasts. I wondered if the Ecology Club might know anything about this epidemic, so I attended a meeting.

People were cordial to me as a visitor to the group, and I listened patiently to plans for Sian Ka'an, the soon-to-be-announced Biosphere for Humanity south of Tulúm. But at last I brought up the issue that had led me to the meeting. I pulled aside the neckline of my blouse to show them a minimally revealing area of bites.

The club members looked at me as if I were a madwoman, as if I were about to undress in front of them. Apparently nobody had understood that I was bringing up a question related to local ecology. I felt horribly embarrassed.

A long time went by before I found out what produced the swatches of welts.

The color of Laguna Nichupte had changed during my time in Cancún. Once I had snorkeled in its transparent water, and tried to hook a lobster I saw on the bottom. Now the lagoon was a muddy khaki color. No one swam or water-skied there anymore. One afternoon on a pier by Lorenzillo's Restaurant in the lagoon, Arturo yelled, "Mamá, look at all the jellyfish!" From where we stood, it seemed the entire lagoon was made up of them, most no bigger than a fingertip. During low tide, I surmised, they must wash into the sea through the channel near Punta Nizuc. Then currents would carry them out into the waves. I must have been swimming among them without feeling their stings. Apparently they liked to get underneath bathing suits and do their business there. I couldn't tell if the welts were bites or reactions to a toxin of some kind; I just knew they left me in misery.

Was this all that was bothering me? No. Now there was plenty of traffic on the way to the beach, and I hated to sit in traffic; it had been one of my reasons for leaving New York. At times it took so long to get to the water, there wasn't enough time left for a diminished run and a scary swim.

Meanwhile Avenue Tulúm, my old stomping grounds, seemed shabbier with each tourist season. Time-share sales people assaulted non-Mexican couples morning and night. I got a laugh out of one tourist's response to a salesman's spiel: "Wait, wait, don't start your pitch," an American told a hawker. Putting an arm around his woman companion, the tourist grinned and announced, "We're not MARRIED!"

Anyway, all up and down the avenue and on the beach, people were selling tee shirts three for ten dollars, and the handicraft markets now specialized in shell jewelry from the Philippines and Cancún souvenirs made in China.

Then there was the new neighbor. As soon as she moved in, she built a second-floor commercial aerobics studio that blocked the breezes my home was designed for. Her studio had a space between walls and roof for ventilation inside, but that meant that the sound of the amplifiers reverberated all over our block. The cardio mixes started blaring at full volume at seven a.m., six days a week. Neighbors and I objected. We suggested that she enclose the open space and install air-conditioning. Finally, we called in the city's noise abatement department. But the aerobics studio owner had connections; nothing we did or said made any difference.

Manolo visited Arturo and me often, but not regularly. If I wanted him to take care of Arturo at a certain time, it was a good bet he wouldn't show. But when I had a date—how did he know it? That was when he would come over, and I'd have to introduce him to the new man I had met.

There were always surprises with Manolo. Once I was driving to the hotel zone when I saw him trying to hitch a ride, wearing my favorite bright yellow cotton shirt, one I'd been looking all over for.

Manolo still came to Xicalango parties, invited or no. His drinking pattern was worse than ever. He'd get seriously drunk after just one or two drinks, and start babbling and threatening. One Halloween party was a nightmare: Manolo showed up fabulously turned out, as usual. He'd made himself a rooster's cockscomb and beak. Dressed only in black Speedo trunks, he had covered his neck and body in feathers. Not long after the drinking and dancing started, he got into a fight out front, and someone called the police. I didn't see it start, but I did see the officers pushing his poor chicken butt into the van and taking him away.

The plan for a financial settlement between Manolo and me was all my idea: since I had paid for the property and the sailboat, and Manolo's contributions toward the construction of our house were small compared to mine, I decided that he could keep La Providencia and I would keep the house. But soon another sad event occurred. Shortly after that Halloween party, Manolo took La Providencia to Isla Mujeres. He anchored the sailboat just outside the neck of the harbor, where there were no fees to pay. That's where the boat sank.

A wooden boat must have a bilge pump with an automatic turn-on mechanism, so that when water in the bilge reaches a certain level, the pump will purge it. The Providencia had such an automatic pump. Still, the captain must keep an eye on the automatic, to make sure its battery is charged. Manolo let it slide, and La Providencia slid right down twenty feet, onto the floor of the channel. I pictured Arturo sitting in his child seat in the cabin, me beside him and Manolo on deck at the helm, sitting up but all of us pale turquoise blue, on the bottom of the sea. It made me sick.

Other reasons for leaving Cancún related to Arturo. He had a preschooler's terrific energy and he rarely seemed sick, but the poor eating and the inflated belly came and went, came and went. Some said treat it aggressively, others said let it go—I didn't know what to do.

There was the language, too. Manolo spoke to Arturo in Spanish, and I spoke to him in English, so he understood the two languages from infancy. But once he started preschool, Arturo only spoke in Spanish. When he was with me in a park, a store, on the street or at a party, I spoke to him in English, and he answered me in Spanish. People would look at us questioningly—were these two mother and child, or what?

Once Arturo told me quite clearly, "Brown people like me speak Spanish, white people speak English." I had many answers to that argument, but they didn't convince him. At a hotel swimming pool one day we saw an African-American boy about Arturo's age speaking English with his parents. I could tell that Arturo couldn't believe his ears.

When Arturo was four, I found a wonderful brand-new preschool for him, a Montessori school with a creative young teacher. Arturo made good friends there and so did I. I thought he'd continue at that school throughout his elementary school years.

But by the second year, *la gente* "nice," the richest families in town, discovered this preschool too. With these powerful allies, the director built a much larger school several kilometers outside of town, and announced an increase in tuition of more than 100 percent.

I was angry about it, and called a meeting at Escuela Xicalango. Nearly every one of the original families attended, and we all felt very positive about our chances of keeping the school affordable. But for some reason, I chickened out of being on the committee that would meet with the director—and the committee met with limited success. Of actions I regret during my time in Cancún, this one is high on the list. I think the tuition was raised ninety-five percent instead of one hundred and five. I didn't want Arturo to continue there.

And every day I wondered if I would ever find another husband. I was now forty or forty-one, and there were few unmarried men in town around my age. Even in the late 'eighties, unfaithful husbands were common but divorcés were rare. I did meet one, a funny and intelligent *yucateco* who had spent years in the states. It took less than a month for me to see that he was another alcoholic. I was not going down that road again.

At Escuela Xicalango I had a good friend, a Mexican-American teacher from California. He had been married many years and even had grandchildren, but I felt so attracted to him I had to devise strategies for hiding it. I would never sit next to him or facing him, because I was afraid he could read my feelings on my face. Would I have to remain single the rest of my life?

The parts of this chapter you have read are what immigration studies call the "push factors." Next come the "pull factors."

When my friend Rivka's daughter was born, Arturo and I spent two weeks with her in Berkeley, California. What a place! There were jazz stations on the radio, well-stocked libraries, and interesting people everywhere. In fact, I had four old friends in Berkeley, including my old travel-companion Sandra. She invited us out sailing in the bay with friends of hers, and what fun that was, maneuvering in the brisk winds, with hip, educated shipmates who paid plenty of attention to me and my cute little one.

Back in Cancún, Arturo and I raved to our friends Leti and Humberto and their son Alex about what we had seen and done in the US. That family was always game for something new. Together we planned a summer driving trip to California, with visits to Mexican ruins and US national parks along the way. Mid-August, Leti's family would fly back to Cancún, while Arturo and I would remain in Berkeley for six months.

That was the plan. On July 31st, with nearly four thousand miles behind us and Humberto at the wheel, the car rocked with cheering when the Bay Bridge hove into sight. I squeezed Arturo tight, as elated as I'd felt entering Cancún thirteen years earlier. Sandra found us a roomy sublet near the University. Six weeks later, in my Portuguese class, I met the daring and multifaceted David. He and I will soon celebrate our twenty-first wedding anniversary and our son Lee's twentieth birthday. It is still an adventure.

In Cancún, Xicalango continued earning well for several years. More time went by during which administrators came and went, yet the school maintained itself. Then came the year when the school secretary called me nearly every pay period, asking me to wire money. I was then working at a California middle school, and the money came out of my public school earnings—I *had* to sell Escuela Xicalango.

Xicalango was bought by a couple who opened a Spanish-language school in its place. That school continues in operation to this day, under one name or another. But no matter what the name, it is still The Place Where the Language Changes.

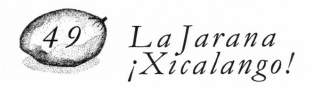

49 La Jarana ¡Xicalango!

This Yucatecan dance tune was written for Escuela Xicalango by student Augusto Assereto. During the period described in this story, Mr. Assereto, a native of Mérida, Yucatán, was well known as a minister, lyricist and composer.

LA JARANA ¡XICALANGO!

Xicalango, escuela de idiomas
que das a nosotros un grato saber
Xicalango, te canto gozoso
Y quiero armonioso en nuevo querer
Compartir alegrías y penas
Propias y ajenas en música ya,
Y dejar a jóvenes fuertes
Muchachas sonrientes prosperando ya
Ejemplares a todas las gentes
Que vean vivientes nueva humanidad.

Xicalango, rinconcito alegre
Con cielo envidiable y flora especial
Xicalango, pedazo de dicha
que con tu sonrisa eres peculiar
Xicalango, siembras en la Nader
Avenida hermosa dentro de Cancún
El saber, que a joven hermosa
La viste de rosa y velo de tul
Ya sea Carmen, Tully o Rosario
Vuélvela primario reina sin igual

XICALANGO JARANA
Translation by Deborah Frisch

Xicalango Academy of Languages
You give us the knowledge that lends our lives joy
Xicalango, I gladly sing to you
Harmoniously, I hope, and with new aspirations
Sharing pleasures and sorrow
With our companions
through the music we sing,
Making us, strong young men and
Smiling young women, prosper,
Examples to everyone
Who recognizes in us
New humanity

Xicalango, happy little corner
With its enviable bright sky and rare flowers
Xicalango, a spot of joy
With your special smile
Xicalango, on Avenue Nader
You clothe a young woman
Be she Carmen, Tully or Rosario
In shining veils of color
Unique, like a true queen.

FIN

For more information about the author and her work, please visit

www.xicalangopress.com
or
www.deborahfrisch.com
or
latinofile.wordpress.com